DD
221.5
.H49413

Hillgruber,
Andreas.

Germany and the
two World Wars

© THE BAKER & TAYLOR CO.

Germany and the Two World Wars

GERMANY
AND THE
TWO WORLD WARS

Andreas Hillgruber

Translated by William C. Kirby

Harvard University Press
Cambridge, Massachusetts
and
London, England
1981

Library of Congress Cataloging in Publication Data

Hillgruber, Andreas.
    Germany and the two World Wars.

    Translation of Deutschlands Rolle in der Vorgeschichte der bei-
den Weltkriege.
    Bibliography: p.
    Includes index.
    1. Germany—Foreign relations—1871–1918.   2. Ger-
many—Foreign relations—1933–1945.   3. European War,
1914–1918—Germany.   4. World War, 1939–1945—Germany.   I. Title.
DD221.5.H49413   327.43   80-27036
ISBN 0-674-35321-8

PREFACE TO THE
1981 EDITION

THIS sketch of Germany's role in the events preceding the two
world wars was written at the suggestion of Werner Conze
of the University of Heidelberg and first appeared in 1967 as
volume 7 in the series The German Question in the World. The
book sought to clarify, by means of a concise exposition and
analysis addressed to a wider reading public interested in history
and politics, the renewed scholarly discussion concerning the
German share of responsibility for the catastrophes of the two
world wars. This discussion was stimulated in the early 1960s
by Fritz Fischer's Germany's Aims in the First World War and
by the books of the American David L. Hoggan and the British
historian A. J. P. Taylor on the origins of the Second World
War.* These works made untenable the belief that one could
sharply differentiate, as Walter Hofer had done, between the
"outbreak" of war in 1914, to which the German government
supposedly contributed no more than the government of any
other European power, and the "unleashing" of war in 1939,
for which Hitler and National Socialist Germany were given full
and almost exclusive responsibility. This newly derived account-

---

* Fritz Fischer, Griff nach der Weltmacht (Düsseldorf, 1961), translated as
Germany's Aims in the First World War (New York, 1967); David L. Hoggan,
Der erzwungene Krieg (Tübingen, 1961); A. J. P. Taylor, The Origins of the
Second World War (London, 1961).

ability of German political leadership for the outbreak of both the first and the second world wars made both the problem of continuity in German foreign policy from Bismarck to Hitler and the question of the quantitative and qualitative comparability of German war aims during 1914–1918 and 1939–1945 central concerns for historical reflection.

The works of Fischer, Hoggan, and Taylor could not have been more different in terms of methodology, critical treatment of new theses, and motivations of the authors. But because they appeared at the same time, readers could not always follow the scholarly debate in its specialized aspects, nor, understandably enough, always discern the relative significance of a given contribution; the antecedents of the first and second world wars and the role of Germany in international politics in the years preceding 1914 and 1939 seemed parallel.

I attempted to provide a treatment that would at least point to the larger perspective that at times threatened to become lost in the scholarly debate. I also sought to clarify the quite different roles played by Germany before the first and second world wars. Above all, I hoped to attribute different degrees of responsibility for the disasters of 1914–1918 and 1939–1945 to the leaders of the German Empire and the National Socialists. Following recent research, but eschewing the scholarly apparatus of numerous notes, I attempted to formulate succinctly the goals, ideas, and "programs" of German foreign policy before the two world wars and, so far as necessary for my purposes, the basic aims of the major opposing powers.

Special attention was given to the intentions, motives, and tactics of the German leadership in making decisions during the crises of July 1914 and August 1939. But a compact survey containing all possible details of the confusing diplomatic maneuvers of the weeks preceding the outbreak of war in 1914 and 1939 was not intended. Rather, of the lines that converged toward July 1914 and August 1939, I brought into the narrative only those that served as paths through the thicket of international politics of the prewar eras: they served only to delineate the context in which decisions were made in July 1914 and August 1939. These conscious limitations of the work were indicated in the original.

An expansion of the narrative from 1939 to 1941 seemed imperative, however. To be sure, September 1939 is the generally accepted time of the unleashing of the Second World War. But this is true only in a qualified sense. In 1914 all the European great powers and Japan took sides in the struggle with only the United States abstaining, but in 1939 as war broke out between Germany, Great Britain, and France following the German attack on Poland, the opposing coalitions were not yet clearly defined. Not even the position of such powers as the Soviet Union and Japan could be predicted.

More important, Hitler conceived of the assault on Poland as merely the first in a series of regionally limited "lightning wars," not the spark to set off a general European war. For him, the decisive war was to have begun only with the attack on the Soviet Union. Thus Hitler's decision to launch the Eastern war, a racial-ideological war of annihilation, had to be included in my account. For only then does the full measure of Nazi Germany's responsibility for the catastrophe of the Second World War emerge with complete clarity. And it is the related introduction of the "final solution"—the extermination of the Jews in the whole of German-controlled Europe—that demonstrates the qualitative difference between Germany's aims in the first and second world wars.

Since 1967, research in areas that are just touched upon here has progressed considerably. A pronounced center of attention —primarily in terms of social history, although with occasional forays into the realm of foreign policy—has been the history of Wilhelmine Germany as seen in the light of intensified research on imperialism. Historical interest in National Socialism, and in the domestic and foreign policies of the Third Reich, has also expanded enormously, from a variety of viewpoints and research strategies. If, as I wrote in the preface to the 1967 edition, it was presumptuous to treat so central a problem in recent German history in so short a space, it is all the more so today, given the quite different state of historical research. If I have nevertheless proceeded to offer here a second edition, the decisive factor is that, despite a profusion of monographs and essays on the outbreak of the First World War and the unleashing and expansion of the second, there has been to date no comparable attempt to discuss and analyze, in a comparative fashion, Germany's role in the events preceding both world wars. Moreover, no other study—as far as I know—has given due emphasis to the direct relationship between the war aims of the Imperial German leadership, as they were radically transformed during the course of the First World War, and the formulation of Hitler's program of expansion.

Like the original, this edition is intended as an introductory work written for the wider public interested in historical and political questions. Revisions have therefore been limited in the second edition to those passages that, because of more recent research, had to be revised. In particular, the interpretation of the crises of July 1914 and the summer of 1939 has remained, like the opinion of this scholar, unchanged.

The bibliography, on the other hand, has been expanded. Still, it makes no claim to be comprehensive, even with respect to the most important titles relevant to the various sections of the text.

Andreas Hillgruber

CONTENTS

Germany and the Two World Wars

1

FROM GREAT POWER POLICY
TO WORLD POLICY

"WE must understand that the unification of Germany was a youthful prank played by the nation in its old age, and one that given the costs, would have been better left undone if it were meant to be the termination, and not the point of departure for a German policy of world power."[1] With these oft-cited words from his inaugural lecture at Freiburg in 1895, Max Weber pointed out the choice facing the German Empire at the outset of the Wilhelmine period. Should it remain satisfied with the position given it by Bismarck as a European great power? That would have meant, at least in the long run, that by abstaining from the competition for colonies among the other European powers, in full swing since the 1870s and 1880s, Germany would fall behind these new "world powers" and lose the position of equality attained in 1866–1871. Or, on the contrary, should the Reich join this race belatedly, with a vengeance, even if this entailed the likelihood of increasing tensions with the other powers?

For Max Weber himself the answer was clear. He was an enthusiastic advocate of resolute power politics in foreign affairs. Weber believed that through liberal domestic reforms—an overdue compromise between the monarchy, the late-feudal-*cum*-bourgeois ruling elite, and the working masses represented by Social Democracy—Germany could only strengthen its ability to pursue an active foreign policy beyond Europe. "National

imperialism, export policy, imperialistic industrial and naval
policies, power politics, and a 'world policy' [*Weltpolitik*] were
inseparable for him."[2]

Weber outlined the grand new goals of German policy at the
outset of what was to prove a prolonged period of economic expansion in which the German liberal upper-bourgeoisie was en-
gulfed by a wave of imperialist agitation. Only now had the
enormous economic potential and the political dynamism of the
nation united by Bismarck revealed themselves. In but a few
years, Germany had become second only to England as a trading
and industrial power. Max Weber's words expressed a growing
sense of power that bewitched first the propertied and educated
classes, then the entire ruling stratum, and finally the nation almost as a whole.

Behind this feeling stood the demand that the Reich, which
had belatedly entered the ranks of the great powers, be considered not only one of the decisive powers of the continent, but
one equal to any in the world, and be allowed to take its place
alongside the established empires. This meant, above all, equal
status with England, whose inspiring achievements served as
both model and measure for Germany. The self-image of Germany, based upon its own accomplishments in all fields, demanded no less. The speeches, proclamations, and marginalia of
Emperor William II, who gave his name to this era of German
history, perhaps best reflect the atmosphere of the two decades
between the beginning of the great economic boom and the catastrophe of the war. Something of the boasting, swaggering
character of this ruler, ever childish, always overawed by the
naturally expanding and seemingly boundless potential of the
German Empire, is revealed in his many celebrated pronouncements.

But what did it mean if, after 1895, all levels of German public opinion discussed a world power role for the Reich? What
concrete aims of the German government lay hidden behind the
glittering, nebulous-sounding phrases about a German world
power policy? What was the relationship in Wilhelmine Germany between economic development, foreign policy, and strategic planning (which as the main spheres of activity of a great
power in the imperialist age were more or less interconnected)?

These are the basic questions that I shall try to elucidate. But first it is necessary to understand the Reich's position in the alignment of powers on entering this new political phase.

Immediately following Bismarck's dismissal in March 1890, and well before the first steps toward a world policy were risked in the wake of the economic recovery of 1894–1895, Germany turned away from the basic (and, toward the last, controversial) lines of Bismarckian foreign policy. The failure to renew the Reinsurance Treaty with Russia marked the break. This was the work of the new political leadership of the empire, and contravened both the desires of the Russian government and the expressed will of William II, who had just declared his intention to take the helm of the Reich into his own hands. I shall investigate this first, fundamental decision of the "New Course" in greater detail, for it shows, at an early date, characteristics that were to typify the conduct of foreign policy in the Wilhelmine period and also reveals the structure of the Reich leadership, where general policy was laid down or, more correctly, ought to have been laid down. The decision is all the more important since one of its direct consequences was a major alteration in the alignment of the European powers.

The decision not to renew the treaty was based upon the foreign policy views of Friedrich von Holstein, privy councillor in the Foreign Ministry, whose opinions contradicted those of Bismarck. Following the "War-in-Sight" crisis of early 1875, which had suddenly revealed the Reich's vulnerable position, Bismarck's policies were based on the principle that the basic goal had to be the creation and maintenance of a European environment "in which all the powers, except France, have need of us, and so far as possible are kept from forming coalitions against us by their relations with each other."[3] By the final years of Bismarck's rule, however, Holstein believed that the basic premise of the Chancellor's policy had become outdated, for war with Russia would be the inevitable result of dynamic Russian activity in the Balkans and steadily mounting pressure on Germany's partner in the Dual Alliance, Austria-Hungary. Holstein was also convinced that any attempt to come to terms with France would succumb to the French claim to Alsace-Lorraine, which had never been renounced.

In fact, Bismarck's mistaken decision (as he himself belatedly recognized) of September 1870 to promote the annexation of Alsace-Lorraine as a German war goal and to continue the Franco-Prussian War on its behalf handicapped subsequent German foreign policy. It ensured that, in case of an Eastern war, France would not idly countenance a German victory over Russia, but would seize the occasion for *revanche*. Nor could a repetition of the Western war of 1870–1871, which was limited to Germany and France, with Russia maintaining benevolent neutrality toward Prussia, now be expected. However the conflict might originate, then, Germany would have to reckon with a continental war on two fronts; a triumph over one of her two great neighbors would transform the semi-hegemonic position in Europe, won by the Reich in 1871, into uncontested hegemony.

Holstein believed that this situation would not threaten the Reich if it were possible—and this had to be the central goal of future policy—to create an alignment of powers in Europe that was favorable in other respects. This meant a close, in effect "unconditional," alliance with Austria-Hungary, expanded through the adherence of Italy to a weightier Triple Alliance. Crucially, such an alliance would have its western as well as its Mediterranean flank shielded by a clear German option for England. Holstein calculated that England would approach the Reich without any special German initiative, if Germany would but take a definitive position in the global political contest between England and Russia, which Holstein saw as a constant, by abandoning the close relationship with Russia that Bismarck had nurtured.

England had to and would "come around." That was the basic conviction. It remained a conviction until the last years before the war, despite the fact that the foundations for even a qualified and circumscribed Anglo-German agreement, perhaps still present at the outset, had by then become questionable. In its core, the argument was that time might be working against Germany and the Triple Alliance in Europe. But on a global scale, time was most certainly working against Britain and its empire, so that England needed German protection of its European interests in the face of its worldwide conflicts with Russia,

France, and especially America. And Britain needed this as much, indeed more than, Germany required English support against the two continental powers, Russia and France.

This conception of foreign policy, which to be sure in the years 1897–1906 was overlaid with another, aggressive, world policy in the Tirpitz Plan, was not a blueprint for dynamic and far-reaching action. Rather, it was predicated upon a fundamental concern with security. Its goals, with their fixed and unalterable premises, were of course geared to a future war, but no conceptions of the nature of this war or its possible outcome were developed. In other words, the dominant concept of Reich policy was not a program of expansion.

It was not Holstein, however, but Bismarck's successor as Chancellor, Count Georg Leo von Caprivi, who was responsible for the critical decision of 1890 that was to define German foreign policy for a considerable period. Caprivi was not one to make up his mind lightly or to be influenced by a desire to accommodate the monarch; William II, after all, wanted the treaty with Russia renewed at all costs. And precisely because this burdensome decision was made by such a serious and conscientious individual, we gain insight here into central elements of the imperial leadership's self-image which transcend the case at hand. Already then, long before the imperialistic exuberance of later years, a marked overestimation of Germany's strength and capacity to gain allies stood in curious juxtaposition to a fatalistic view of future European developments, in which war between Germany and Russia (and France too) was unavoidable, despite all efforts to the contrary.

Bismarck in his contingency planning had never renounced war as the *ultima ratio* of foreign policy. Yet the difference between his view and that of his successors—including, significantly, the most conscientious among them, Caprivi and Bethmann Hollweg—is obvious. Unlike them, Bismarck did not view war as something fated, to which a statesman must submit if he saw no alternative in performing the task entrusted to him: the maintenance of the great power position won by the Reich in Europe in 1870–1871. War, to Bismarck, was the statesman's ultimate weapon and responsibility, to be entered into as a result of independent decision, in order to attain an objective that was deemed essential. These two fundamentally different attitudes toward the phenomenon of war determined, each in its time, the orientation of foreign policy.

Bismarck's prodigious accumulation of seemingly contradictory alliances with various powers after 1875 was neither intended, nor suited, for war. His premise was that the preservation of Germany's great power status required keeping the general European peace. After 1890, this axiom was replaced by another that supposed rigid fronts and unbridgeable differences between certain great powers and was concerned with strengthening the German position through clear alliances. Foreign policy thereby became increasingly one-dimensional and acquired, more or less necessarily, an ever stronger strategic, and at length, narrowly military, emphasis.

Bismarck's successors possessed neither the intellectual superiority nor the skills of statecraft, developed over the course of long political experience, that were needed to ensure that the Chancellor would maintain control of all aspects of national policy. Because of the dualistic structure of the Reich leadership —a drastic cleavage between the political and military areas— the central position of the Chancellor was less an institution than a Bismarckian accomplishment. Bismarck's successors found themselves subject instead to diverse pressures in both domestic and foreign policy and restricted by a variety of circumstances and checks. Most of all, they simply did not have the authority, and did not win the power, to make good their political claims to leadership vis-à-vis the military bureaucracy. They could not, as Bismarck had done with the aid of William I and in constant conflict with Moltke, gain the acceptance of a military strategy consonant with their foreign policy. William II failed in the task that was properly his as constitutional monarch: the integration of the civil and military components into a coherent general policy. Thus the complementary and conflicting responsibilities of the political leadership and Foreign Ministry on the one hand, and general staff, Prussian War Ministry, and (especially later) the naval secretary on the other, were characteristic of the lack of unified direction of German policy in the Wilhelmine era.

In the 1890s, William II toyed with the idea of a coup d'état to destroy domestic opposition, in particular Social Democracy, and to rally together divergent power groups under his personal leadership. But in the following years he became increasingly resigned to his position, completely so after the "Daily Telegraph affair" of 1908 shook his self-esteem. The traditional claim of the Prussian military to a privileged position in the state—grounded in the historically problematic military geography of Prussia (and the Reich) in the center of Europe, now exacerbated by advances in military technology and the growing vulnerability of modern industrial states to hostile action on their territory—made it exceedingly likely that, without an overpowering statesman such as Bismarck to lead firmly and keep the military in bounds, military perspectives would override political concerns when Reich policy was set in times of crisis.

The first important foreign policy decision of the New Course, the nonrenewal of the Reinsurance Treaty with Russia, strengthened the tendency to make military strategy the axis on which foreign policy deliberations would turn. Just as irreconcilable differences with France after 1871 had severely limited Germany's latitude in making alliances—on which it was more dependent than other nations because of its central geographic position—so the deliberate severing of the Russian connection, which eventually resulted in a Franco-Russian alliance directed exclusively against Germany, constrained the Reich to become preeminently concerned with rectifying its oppressive strategic predicament.

Since the founding of the Reich, the general staff had believed this two-front pressure to be unavoidable. Beginning with Field Marshal Helmuth von Moltke's studies and campaign plans for a possible war against Russia and France in the Spring of 1871, it was the starting point for all operational deliberations. But the decisive difference with the period after 1890 was that Bismarck, through his enormously complicated alliances, had continually endeavored to ensure that such a war would never take place. The new Reich leadership, however, was willing to lower its sights and base its foreign policy on the expectation of that very war, which, at all odds, German diplomacy could not prevent.

The difficult transition from Bismarck's to Holstein's foreign policy was aggravated by a fundamental, though coincidental, shift in the operational plans of the general staff, a temporal conjunction of two independent lines of development. Advances in armaments technology, the continued modernization of the French military establishment, and an improvement of Russian defenses in Poland all threatened Germany's chances of victory in both east and west and led to a reversal of the planned sequential order of German operations in case of war with Russia and France. This switch was the work of Count Alfred von Schlieffen, chief of the general staff from 1891 to 1905. Because of increasing doubt that Russia could be dealt a decisive blow in a matter of weeks, allowing the Reich to then concentrate on France—as Moltke had still envisioned it in the last years of Bismarck's rule—there remained but one alternative: to seek a military victory first in the west and then deal with the east.

Schlieffen assumed that the rapid elimination of France at the outset of war was an absolute necessity. And to achieve thoroughgoing success in the west, a march by the right flank of the German army through Belgium was deemed unavoidable. The plan was worked out in its essence in 1891, and fully by 1897. Given the well known English interest in Belgian neutrality, this strategy implied a confrontation with England too, although this was concealed in peacetime. According to the foreign policy of the New Course, Germany sought alliance, not conflict with England, but military strategy now coerced foreign policy unequivocally. To be sure, the weighty, indeed catastrophic, political consequences of the new operational plan, still undergoing elaboration, remained hidden from the Reich leadership for many years, particularly during the administrations of Chancellors Hohenlohe (1894–1900) and Bülow (1900–1909). Then, in contrast to the Caprivi period, a certain optimism prevailed concerning further political developments in Europe. Their era was filled with the illusions of German world power.

Despite the fluctuations of day-to-day politics and the serious Anglo-German colonial rivalry in Africa that began in 1895–1896 with enormous negative impact on the political climate (mirrored thereafter in the undying polemics of the German and British presses), the years before the turn of the century were marked by the hope on the part of the German political leadership that, sooner or later, England would make the advances toward Germany that had been expected since 1890. It was felt that a continuation of Britain's "splendid isolation" was no longer possible in an era of increasing tensions with her great colonial rivals: Russia in East and Central Asia, and France in Africa. In the German view of English interests, a decision for alignment with Germany, with which England had relatively few outstanding conflicts, was inherently logical. And the Reich government pursued this goal with ever more daring tactics: with enticement, pressure, and threats. Even temporary cooperation with Russia and France during the Sino-Japanese War of 1894–1895 was ultimately intended only to make Germany an attractive ally for Britain.

In the decade before the turn of the century, however, there had already developed a gradual (thus almost imperceptible) but profound estrangement between Germany and most other nations of a kind that, with the benefit of historical hindsight, can be said never to have existed during the Bismarckian period. This was a consequence of the methods of German foreign policy in the Wilhelmine era and even more of the accompanying commentary of German public opinion. Public opinion in other European nations slowly came to sense a threat, less because of the goals of German foreign policy per se than the crude, overbearing style that Germany projected on the international stage. Without this background, one cannot understand the truly radical hate for Germany and all things German that broke out in the Entente countries with the war of 1914.

The second fundamental decision of the Wilhelmine era, after the nonrenewal of the Russian treaty, was inaugurated by Admiral Alfred von Tirpitz with the two naval bills of 1898 and 1900: the building of a fleet. With its global offensive thrust, the Tirpitz Plan was in a political sense a sharp departure from Holstein's New Course. The projected grand fleet was publicly touted as a "risk fleet," the risk being in the time needed to build it, after which it would theoretically serve to deter England. But it was also built to defeat English sea power in a war, should England fail to meet German conditions for an alliance. Until the fleet was completed, Tirpitz felt, Germany ought to come to terms with neither Britain nor Russia. He pleaded for restraint in foreign policy. But Prince Bernhard von Bülow, who had become Foreign Secretary in 1897 and Chancellor in 1900, disagreed. He sought instead a *rapprochement* with Russia in order to join her at a future date in "turning the tables" on the British Empire and thus taking "possession of the rich colonial inheritance."

Yet the danger zone that Tirpitz warned would continue pending completion of the fleet was by no means past when England introduced the dreadnought battleship in 1906. This was an apparent success for German naval policy, since it reduced the significance of England's numerical superiority in ships of the line and thus cut down overnight the numerical gap between the British and German fleets. In truth it spelled the failure of Tirpitz's plan and the expansionist notions that had been based on it. It was then unavoidable that German foreign policy would retreat to the basic lines of continental policy. But because of the propagandistic selling of the fleet and the German public's illusions concerning a world policy, this fact was never admitted. The discrepancy between the public's expectations and the real opportunities open to the Reich grew ever larger.

The aim of gaining England as an ally and still more the decision to build a world class fleet certainly made the foreign policy of the New Course appear global in scope. But as a world policy, Germany's incessant activity—or better, busyness—all over the world was more irritating than successful. We need only remember Germany's stand during the Sino-Japanese War of 1894–1895; the Krüger telegram of 1896; the Samoan conflict with Britain and the United States in 1898–1899; the intervention in the Spanish-American War with the curious naval expedition to Manila in 1898; and finally, the vain attempt to lead the suppression of the Boxer Rebellion in China in 1900. After the turn of the century, this fumbling in diverse arenas and political hotspots was followed—with important consequences for overall German policy before 1914—by a gradual concentration on winning strong economic, military, and political influence in the Near East, particularly in the Ottoman Empire with the Berlin to Baghdad Railroad as the central project.

And yet even in this period, policy was directed toward continental Europe. In view of the security needs of Germany and Austria-Hungary against the newly consummated Franco-Russian alliance (1894), the goal was still to win England around. This was nowhere more evident than during the Anglo-German alliance negotiations of 1898–1901. Then, for a time, England pursued a world policy in the literal sense, seeking partnership with Germany outside of Europe, particularly in East Asia, for the sake of a common Anglo-German confrontation with Russia at the risk of war over China. It was, however, a partnership in which Germany was relegated to the position of junior partner; and German statesmen, despite all the uncoordinated, unprogrammatic overseas actions that they passed off pompously as "world policy," were in the last analysis solely concerned with improving Germany's position in Europe. That is why Holstein obdurately insisted on treaty guarantees binding England to the Triple Alliance. But England and Germany had fundamentally dissimilar interests: England's being those of "a world power that sought relief on the periphery of its empire," and Germany's those of "a European great power forced to secure the nucleus of its existence in Europe."[4] This was the objective root of Anglo-German tension and the reason for the failure of the negotiations.

Behind the dispute over a treaty and the form it would take was Germany's determination to enter into alliance with England only as a politically equal sovereign great power and, moreover, as a world power—a status Germany already enjoyed in the economic sense. No junior partnership was acceptable. Of course, looking back now, we may perceive that because of her position in Central Europe, rendered increasingly unfavorable by the development of military technology, only the role of junior partner in association with one of the truly global powers would have been appropriate in the long run. The Reich found itself encircled in Central Europe in two ways: in the narrow sense, squeezed between the great powers, France and Russia (of which the latter possessed the natural, that is, the spatial, demographic, economic, and geographic preconditions for becoming a world power), and in a wider sense blockaded by the established sea and world power, England, behind which America was developing as a potential world power.

At that time, however, such an insight would have required an uncommon amount of political acumen and self-restraint, both of which directly contradicted the spirit of the imperialist epoch in general and the Wilhelmine period in Germany in particular. A voluntary retreat by Germany into the ranks of the lesser powers could hardly be expected of German statesmen, all of whom were strongly obsessed with the theme of great power prestige and none of whom possessed remarkable stature— quite aside from the fact that most of the nation, including to a limited degree the Social Democrats, believed that Germany *had* to become an independent world power. Whatever else it might mean, that term meant equality with England. The Reich tried to conceal the disparity between reality and pretension by pursuing an old-style European policy in "world-political" terms. In truth, what always mattered first and foremost was the security of the German position in Central Europe.

The same desire to maintain full freedom of maneuver in both foreign policy and military strategy determined the attitude of the Reich leadership at the two Hague Conferences of 1899 and 1907. There the first attempts were made to establish compulsory arbitration of international disputes and an international court, and—especially—to reach agreement on steps leading to general disarmament. To the Reich leadership, however, treaties to limit arms and force nations to the bar of arbitration robbed Germany of that weapon "on which, in her central position, she must rely in time of crisis: her superior military organization, which affords her a headstart in any general mobilization and which may well prove decisive."[5] This was doubtless an honest conviction, based on centuries of actual or imagined practice by great powers. But it rejected out of hand the possibility of redefining conventional power politics by entering into new forms of international political behavior, and did so without ever seriously examining the opportunities involved, particularly for the hard-pressed German situation.

We may reserve the question of whether this might have been an escape from the cul-de-sac in which German foreign policy found itself. Suffice it to note that even though other governments followed the systematic German opposition at the Hague Conferences item by item, the obstinate attitude of the Reich leadership at the Hague led Germany into a further, moral, isolation in the eyes of Europe.

2

THE RETURN
OF THE GREAT POWERS
TO EUROPE

T HE fateful implications of Tirpitz's fleet for German policy
first became fully apparent with the Russo-Japanese War of
1904–1905, which was the turning point in the development of
international relations in the period between 1890 and 1914.
The crucial effect of the East Asian war on Europe was a change
in England's perception of the relative weight of Russia and Germany in the European balance of power. Despite criticism of
elements of German foreign policy, the British government had
heretofore never seen the Reich as an absolute threat to the European system. Russia and France had been perceived as strong
—at times overly strong—counterweights to Germany and
Austria-Hungary in Europe and, moreover, as England's chief
rivals overseas. Russia's defeat by Japan was as unexpected as it
was grave, exposing in their entirety the weaknesses of the czarist regime and its army. Further, the Russian East Asian fleet,
which was to counterbalance the German navy, had been wiped
out and would play no role for a long time to come. To the English, then, Russia would not be a significant factor in European
power politics for the foreseeable future. This lent Germany a
threatening preponderance, so that henceforth Britain's primary
interest was in supporting Germany's continental opponents.

The English government maintained this assessment of the
strength of the two foremost continental powers until 1914. It
thus followed that in case of war, only immediate British inter-

vention against Germany could hinder a German victory over France and a debilitated Russia. Failing that, German continental hegemony was assured.

The world war of 1914–1918 proved the British estimate of Russian vulnerability correct. Yet despite similar initial assessments by the general staff and the political leadership under Bethmann Hollweg (after 1909), Germany took the renewed growth of Russian strength after the Bosnian crisis (1908–1909) very seriously, indeed to the point of exaggeration. The Reich suffered from the nightmarish fear of being crushed by Russia, or of being pulverized between the millstones of France and Russia, or, even without war, of being paralyzed and ultimately checkmated in its strategic and foreign policies. Social Darwinist images of boundless Russian growth merged with *völkisch* conceptions of the unbridgeable gap between "Slavdom" and "Germandom"—concepts present in the minds of the German leadership even before the turn of the century. These, together with the mechanistic, numerical obsession of the general staff with Russian armaments, led to the same fatal conclusion that Germany was in an increasingly untenable position.

English fear of Germany following the Russo-Japanese War soon led to a far-reaching change in the alignment of the European powers. Although the *entente cordiale* between England and France was understood to be but a partial adjustment of interests in North Africa at its outset in April 1904, that is, shortly after the outbreak of the Asian war, it rapidly developed, in fact if not in law, into a defensive alliance of the two powers whose full impact was not evident in peacetime. It would come into play almost automatically, however, even without specific treaty provisions, in defense of England's vital interests in the event of German military action against France, or—at the very latest—should France's defeat seem imminent. Given Russia's relative demise, the English assumed that a Franco-German war would indeed result in a German victory, with the occupation of French harbors by the German fleet endangering England's very existence—far as such strategic considerations were from Tirpitz's thoughts. Such then were the decisive military and political consequences of the German fleet's construction.

The relative strength of the British and German fleets thus acquired critical importance, and so began the naval arms race between England and Germany that lasted until 1912. Under Tirpitz's commanding influence, Germany persisted in the illusion that England would eventually have to draw in its horns and enter into the alliance of equals that Germany had sought since 1890, even though the race was already lost with England's introduction of the dreadnought.

The German navy's perceptions of this arms race were set down in a memorandum by Vice Admiral Eduard von Capelle, the closest associate of Tirpitz, at the height of the competition in the autumn of 1911:

> England can sustain the competition less than we, as she is tied to the "two keels standard." . . . We, not England, have the trumps in our hand. We need but wait patiently until our current naval bill is completed [that is, until 1917] . . . England must, and in the course of the next few years will, opt for Germany and against France, because it is in England's express interest to do so . . . England must and will come around to us . . . The naval policy is the great achievement of His Majesty's government. Were it to be crowned by an alliance with England, our full potential and military equality would be guaranteed, and a first great success won. If, on the other hand, only a *societas leonina* emerges, then the naval policy will have been a fiasco, and history will so judge it.[1]

Tirpitz's agent in the German embassy in London, Naval Attaché Widenmann, was later of the opinion that, "in the years from 1908 to 1911 we experienced a kind of latent war with England."[2]

The shift in the European balance of power brought about by Russia's drastic decline produced, with the Anglo-German naval race, a steadily growing concentration of the most important elements of the British fleet in the North Sea. This in turn reinforced the ongoing contraction of the "grand policy" of the powers to the European scene and led to a diminution and downplaying of overseas conflicts between them. The final effect was to overemphasize tensions in Europe. The world political situation had thus reversed itself in the few years since the turn of the century. Alliances were not contemplated in terms of the conflict between great global empires, but grew, as they had in the pre-imperialist era, out of the European context. German foreign policy ought to have been mainly concerned with keeping England preoccupied by her overseas interests in Africa and the Near and Far East. This is precisely what Tirpitz's influence on all aspects of German policy, which reached its peak in the years 1908–1912, prevented. The German fleet had such decisive significance in international politics in the decade before the First World War not because of its intrinsic military worth, but because it tied England to Europe. The naval policy increasingly constricted the room in which German foreign policy could maneuver.

To the British government, the danger of German military action against France was particularly great in the years 1904–1905. Russia was then engaged against Japan and, following her defeat, incapable of military action for some time. In response to the perceived threat, England determined to give France unconditional protection, for as the English saw it, a French defeat must result in German hegemony on the continent—a hegemony that appeared half achieved already by virtue of Russia's current impotence. On the German side, however, even though the Schlieffen Plan was finalized in the strategically favorable situation of December 1905, no one responsible for Reich policy was planning a war of conquest or a preventive war against France. To be sure, during the first Moroccan crisis, which the German government deliberately exaggerated to attain a tactical and political objective, Holstein declared that "we must, with all our energy and with a resolve that should not falter come what may, burst apart the ring of the other great powers before it strangles us."[3] But Holstein was convinced that this result could be forced without war, by energetic overtrumping in the diplomatic card game.

The Moroccan crisis was the last attempt by the Reich leadership to maneuver England into a reconciliation with Germany by purely political means. The supposedly foolproof method by which this was to be accomplished was the formation of a continental bloc of Germany, Russia, and France; an intimidated England would then rapidly come to an understanding with Germany. Russia's involvement in the Japanese war and her resultant interest in protecting her European flank seemed a favorable point of departure for the realization of this plan. And in fact, Czar Nicholas II agreed to a surprise initiative of William II and signed a draft treaty at Björkö in July 1905. Since the key Russian ministers could not be won to the cause, however, no serious effort was begun to enlist Russian help in bringing France into the scheme.

In Germany's original calculation, the Moroccan crisis was to be the lever by which France would be separated from England and brought over to the Russo-German grouping. As noted, this complicated game was but a means to impress England with Germany's capacity to make alliances and with its attractiveness as a partner. It failed utterly. What emerged with striking clarity from the Algeciras Conference that ended the Moroccan crisis was not the success of German efforts, but the isolation of Germany and Austria-Hungary. The next attempt to push England into accommodation was neither political nor diplomatic, but took the form of the aforementioned arms race of 1908–1911.

It must be emphasized that it was not in the singularly favorable context of 1905, but in the extraordinarily dangerous situation of 1914 that the German government risked a great war through local military action. In the last analysis, the failure to act in 1905 resulted from the realization that even then, when the Reich was free of the pressures of a two-front war and could amass all her land forces in the west without fear of danger from the rear, victory was probably still unobtainable. Not even the defeat of France was certain; according to Schlieffen's memorandum of December 1905, at least eight additional army corps were needed. But even if the "colossal gamble"[4] were to lead to the desired success, the annihilation of the French army between Paris and the Jura mountains of Switzerland, and France were driven from the field, England remained. With the fleet still under construction, it was doubtful that Germany's forces were sufficient to make the unconquerable island-nation amenable to peace by taking such "pawns" as Belgium, the Netherlands, and Denmark. Compromise with Germany would have entailed English recognition of an unmistakable shift in the European balance to Germany's favor, even if France were to regain full sovereignty.

Thus Germany's military and strategic predicament was clear

even in this best of all possible alignments. Even then, the
Schlieffen Plan was anything but a formula for victory. Rather,
it was dubious strategy in a *vabanque* game played out in a political, military, and strategic situation that sober analysis had
already seen to be hopeless. But Germany's flash of insight in
1905–1906 into its own dilemma, its inability to sustain its
world policy pretensions apart from a temporarily favorable position in Europe, was subsequently repressed again, receding behind a problem deemed once again more crucial after 1909, the
survival of the Reich in a two-front continental war against
France and Russia.

Following the conquest of the remaining unpartitioned areas
of the world by England, Russia, and France (all aided by their
positions on the periphery of Europe), Germany, although in
traditional European terms a great power, was demonstrably
not a world power by the standards of the imperialist age. This
had been proven in a political sense during the alliance negotiations with England at the turn of the century and in the military
realm by the events of 1905. Moreover, Germany had not the
slightest chance of defeating *the* world power, England. If for no
other reason, Germany was therefore not a prospective ally for
England on terms of equal partnership. Nevertheless, Germany
was already an economic world power. This glaring discrepancy
between economic and political power obstructed a clear, realistic judgment by the political and military leadership of the
Reich.

The period after 1905 was shaken by international crises as
the Reich leadership pursued a foreign policy that hovered on
the brink of war. Writing to Prince Bülow in the Spring of 1915,
Bethmann Hollweg recalled this as "a policy of extreme risk, increasing with each repetition."[5] Policy was at bottom no longer
concerned, as in 1895–1904, with the encirclement of a ficti-
tious German world power position, still less with any territorial
expansion on the continent or abroad. At stake now was the
preservation of the position won in 1866 and 1870–1871, Germany's status as a European great power, which was, of course,
the mainstay of German industry's international role. As a result
of the renewed concentration of world politics on Europe, this
defensive effort took place in an international environment that

was rapidly becoming unfavorable to the Reich and its Austro-Hungarian partner, itself beset by internal paralysis and disintegration.

The Anglo-Russian settlement of 1907 did not settle all questions outstanding between those powers, notably the old areas of tension in the Balkans and the Turkish straits. Accordingly, this was not an intimate community of interests such as existed between England and France after 1904–1905. But the delineation of spheres of influence between England and Russia in the Middle East and, indirectly, in East Asia tangibly relieved tensions in those areas and thereby further shifted the weight of "grand policy" to Europe.

Tirpitz's naval competition with England and the related, ill-fated attempt to gain political equality and alliance with England reinforced the Reich's isolation in Europe. That isolation was complete by the time Theobald von Bethmann Hollweg took office as Chancellor in 1909. Bethmann Hollweg sought to achieve a gradual *rapprochement* with England by reducing the naval competition, which domestically meant limiting Tirpitz's still decisive influence on Reich policy. He proposed to loosen the rigid power blocs by a trial collaboration with Britain in specific cases that, if successful, could be extended to all Europe and overseas. At the same time, a disengagement of England from Russia would reduce the perceived Russian threat to Germany and Austria-Hungary.

This approach to foreign policy was diametrically opposed to that of Admiral Tirpitz, and Bethmann Hollweg gained acceptance of it only slowly. When the British War Minister, Lord Haldane, visited Berlin amid great optimism in February 1912, these mutually exclusive policies all but ensured the failure of the Chancellor's efforts to redefine the Anglo-German relationship. Only after March 6, 1912, did matters begin to go Bethmann's way. When the Kaiser, with Tirpitz's prodding, wished to respond to Britain's strengthening of her North Sea fleet by threatening war, Bethmann submitted his resignation. The startled Kaiser refused it.

In his letter of resignation, Bethmann Hollweg set forth his judgment of the responsibility of the German leadership should it decide on war. His statement is useful in judging his conduct during the July crisis of 1914: "If war is forced upon us, we shall fight it and, with God's help, survive. But for ourselves to conjure up a war when neither our honor nor our vital interests have been threatened, this I would take to be an offense against German destiny, even if we could confidently expect total victory."[6] In the terms "honor" and "vital interests," the protection of the Reich's great power status won in 1866 and 1870–1871 found its contemporary expression.

Meanwhile, Russia's submission to a German ultimatum in the Bosnian crisis of 1908–1909 had proved a Pyrrhic victory for the Central Powers. At the height of the crisis, Russian War Minister Roediger had to confess to the czar that his army was incapable of defending the borders, let alone intervening in a conflict in Southeastern Europe. Hence Russia had no choice but to accept a shift in the Balkan balance to Austria's favor. This severe political defeat of the czarist empire signaled, however, the beginning of systematic efforts to overcome the setback of 1909, to transform it into the political gain so necessary for Russian prestige. The army was promptly strengthened and political and military pressure applied to improve the Russian position in the Turkish straits and the Balkans.

The straits thus became a zone of dangerous tension between Russian and German interests, since Germany remained strongly engaged in the Ottoman Empire. It was as if Germany had thrust itself in between the Russian and British spheres of influence in the Eastern Mediterranean and taken over the traditional British contest with Russia there. But in the Balkans the interests of Russia, Austria-Hungary, and Germany were now at odds all three ways. This foreclosed a return to what Bismarck had considered his "last resort": as he admitted in 1895, he had, in the great crises of the 1880s, contemplated "purchasing Russian neutrality at the last minute by abandoning Austria and thereby handing over the Orient to the Russians."[7]

Following Bethmann Hollweg's strategy, German diplomats acted in concert with England during the two Balkan wars (1912–1913) to keep the Russian comeback in the Balkans to a minimum. This cooperation also somewhat reduced the danger of general war, which had grown enormously with the spread of the arms race to the land forces of the powers. Bethmann Holl-

weg believed that persistence on this course could lead to fundamental change, from a compromise in the colonial area (an
Anglo-German Agreement on the Belgian Congo and the Portuguese colonies in Africa was drawn up and for all practical purposes divided the region between the two powers) to the settlement of long-standing differences over the Baghdad Railroad.
The hope was that developments, ever less favorable to the
Reich and its solitary, weak, and willful ally, could thus be
stemmed and German foreign policy regain a degree of flexibility.

The sudden shift from an atmosphere of moderate détente to
a critically restricted position of the Reich, which was so evident
in July 1914, began in late 1913 with the crisis over German influence in the Ottoman Empire, which was sparked by the
Liman von Sanders military mission to Constantinople. This in-
vigorated a previously cautious Russian policy aimed at erecting
an anti-Habsburg confederation in the Balkans and, on the level
of "grand policy," tightening the slackened tie with England
through an Anglo-Russian naval convention along the lines of
the maritime discussions between England and France. Russia's
activity both endangered the Austrian position in the Balkans
and threatened the Reich's leading role in Turkey.

3

THE GERMAN LEADERSHIP
IN THE CRISIS
OF JULY 1914

How did Chancellor von Bethmann Hollweg envisage the total European setting at the outset of 1914, before the intensification of the Balkan situation? What possibilities did he see for German foreign policy? A certain amount of relevant information may be gleaned from a work by his confidential adviser Kurt Riezler, published as "Basic Characteristics of Present Day World Politics" under the pseudonym Ruedorffer.[1] Riezler not only analyzed the international situation, but also developed a theory by which the German leadership might utilize diplomatic crises to gain limited objectives. From the developments of the previous ten years, particularly the behavior of the European powers during the Balkan wars of 1912–1913, Riezler concluded that although the great powers sought in principle to extend their power at the expense of their rivals, they were now increasingly concerned with "postponing military conflict."[2] The "politics of postponement," which worked to avoid a great military collision between the power blocs was, Riezler believed, the result of the continuing possibility of "parallel expansion" by the powers overseas, of the growing interrelation of their economic interests, especially those of England and Germany (the British Empire was after all the principal consumer of German exports), but above all of the destructive nature of modern war. War now threatened a state's very existence. The human and

material losses would be staggering for both victor and van-
quished: "By all estimates, a lost war against any great power
means political ruin for any other great power unless special circumstances intercede—for example if non-participants move
the victor to exceptional forbearance" or if the foreseeable postwar situation makes it appear advisable to all participants to
cease hostilities. From this disparity between risk and gain "only
Russia, and then only in the best of circumstances, may be ex-
cepted. With its great size and endurance, Russia might be im-
mune to national ruin; in defeat it has to fear at most the victory
of revolution and a delay in its development."

Nevertheless, Riezler believed that all great powers viewed
coexistence as a prelude to conflict. Armaments represented the
"modern form of postponement," and so the maintenance of
the arms balance preserved the peace. "Wars are no longer
fought, but calculated." Calculations established the advantages
that a power might gain from an international crisis. "Cannons
may not fire, yet they speak in negotiations." "The greater the
armaments, the greater the discrepancy between the advantages
and disadvantages of war in favor of the latter, and thus in favor
of peace." Riezler's conclusion was that "wars between the
great powers [would] no longer be started because of the rewards to be gained from them, but only from necessity."

The credibility of the threat of war became central to all political activity. Bluff was now the *sine qua non* of diplomacy.
"When two parties dispute and neither wants war, the victor
will not always be the more powerful, that is, the one who can
best endure war, but the one who can longest perpetuate the belief that it is ready to fight—the one with more calm, compo-
sure, tenacity and suppleness." Of course these practices also enhanced the danger of war: "If a government, misled by the
methods of bluff, dares too far, or as we say bluffs itself into a
corner, then retreat may no longer be possible even if it were the
objectively correct policy. Personal interests, rulers' ambitions,
or an expected storm of indignation by nationalists can all bring
about a war that objective interests alone might never justify.
The danger of war in our time lies, therefore, in the domestic
politics of nations in which a weak government faces a strong
nationalist movement."

Changes in the system of alliances represented to Riezler further attempts to twist calculations to one's own advantage. It was fortunate for the cause of peace that there existed "conflicting interests only between individual powers of the Triple Entente and individual powers of the Triple Alliance." In none of the regional zones of tension were *all* the powers equally engaged.

"The very fact of unequal strength in a dispute is enough," Riezler believed, "to occasion the less interested ally to seek to avoid open conflict." Because there was no possibility of altering power relationships on a large scale without a calamitous war, and since whole sections of Europe had already been drawn into firm political camps, the energies of the great powers were directed toward those few areas that Riezler assumed still allowed for a relatively free play of forces. The most conspicuous of these regions was the Balkans. A limited "shift" there "should only be taken seriously when it is already a *fait accompli* and cannot be undone by force." This being so, "policy should be preeminently concerned with avoiding the use of force as far as possible, and to shift the decision for war to the enemy. The decision is grave, more grave than in any time known to history. In all likelihood the enemy will not take it, if all that is at stake is a small alteration of the balance of power that does not affect its vital interests." To Riezler, the real concern for the government of a great power allied only with a stagnating ("stand-still") power—as the German Empire was with Austria-Hungary—was the slow, almost imperceptible shift in the relative power between the two alliance systems that resulted from the waxing military, economic, and, in Riezler's words, "moral" strength of the "aspiring" powers of the two blocs. One had, then, to make a sharp distinction between "rising" and "stagnating" powers. The former could let time work for them. The latter could only try to keep the enemy at bay with the bluff theory of diplomacy and, following a policy of calculated risk in those areas that still allowed for maneuver, to counteract the ultimately negative trend. The diplomacy of a stagnating power, like that of the great power allied to it, consequently became "less settled, more nervous and more variable" than that of states with time on their side. But if the bloc hindered by a "stand-still" power were to forego all attempts at success, and in time of crisis shrink from any risk of war, then the triumph of those powers that could let time do their work was inevitable. "As well as can be foreseen, under such circumstances final victory will belong to the powers with the greatest national strength."

With this conclusion Riezler alluded to the steady, dynamic growth of Russian power that sooner or later would make a struggle between "Slavdom" and "Germandom" unavoidable. In this Riezler shared with Bethmann Hollweg an opinion wide-spread in Europe, particularly in the educated classes of Germany, which can only partially be explained by incredible ignorance about Russia. Just how firmly Bethmann Hollweg held to this notion is strikingly evident from a private conversation in 1912 with von Flatow, later Ambassador to Rome: "Gazing at the park in Hohenfinow, he doubted whether it was worth-while to plant new trees, since the Russians would be there in a few years anyway."[3] To the Chancellor, the Russian triumph might be delayed by regional gains on the part of the Central Powers, but in the long run it could not be denied.

It still seemed possible, however, to stem the "moral" decay and dwindling prestige of the Danubian monarchy by taking decisive action in a relatively propitious crisis situation. The last such victory had been in the Bosnian crisis of 1908–1909, when Russia yielded to the pressure of the Central Powers. Since then, however, developments had taken quite a different turn. In the two Balkan wars of 1912–1913, the initiative had clearly passed to the Russian side. Russia's advantage here had been its ability to shift the balance to its favor by the actions of smaller allies while Russia remained aloof from the military conflicts in order to participate "freely" with other powers in the peace settlements. After 1915, if Russia's preponderance in the Balkans, which had grown threatening following the Liman von Sanders crisis, were to be overcome, then the local balance had first to be altered in favor of a pro-Austrian coalition. Efforts to do just that were in progress, both in Germany and in Austria-Hungary. Yet it remained doubtful that diplomacy alone could do the job. As a "stagnating" power, beset by increasing moral feebleness (in

Riezler's sense), Austria-Hungary had first to prove itself again to be a full-fledged great power, capable of rendering effective support to would-be Balkan allies.

So it was that an Austrian show of power against Serbia, the center of South Slav agitation, seemed imperative at the next opportunity. Because the Central Powers could not improve their position in the Balkans through local allies, as Russia could, Austria-Hungary had to take action itself. The greater risk of a general war, which according to Riezler's theory such action entailed, could be accepted because Austro-Russian differences in the Balkans were of unequal importance to the other great powers. The expectation was that a limited objective would be attained through the mediation of other powers, especially England and Germany. A new Balkan arrangement would then result, and this time—unlike 1912–1913—it would come at Russia's expense and redound to Austria's (and indirectly, Germany's) benefit. The mediation by third powers should not begin too soon, that is, before a real success had been achieved; rather, the bluff theory would permit the exact calculation of how far the crisis should be intensified. The belief that a major war could be avoided was grounded in Riezler's theory that no great power would go to war over a "small shift which does not concern the vital interests" of another great power.[4] Moreover, it was well known that Russian armaments were not scheduled to reach maximum strength until 1917; thus the Russian army could not be considered ready for a major war in 1914. Whereas the improvement of Anglo-German relations in 1912–1913 could only enhance the chances of Austria-Hungary's success, any strengthening of the ties between England and the Franco-Russian alliance would seriously jeopardize them. Indeed, when it became known in mid-June 1914 that England and Russia were negotiating a naval convention in the aftermath of the Liman von Sanders crisis, this loomed as an ominous possibility threatening to alter the entire European situation.

Bethmann Hollweg's policy of seeking an Anglo-German *rapprochement,* at once the background and basis for the Balkan calculations, was not pursued with the goal of disengaging England from the Triple Entente in order to allow a continental war of Germany and Austria-Hungary against France and Russia. According to the strategic viewpoint of the chief of the general staff, the younger Moltke, the prerequisite for such a war was lacking. The Chancellor's objective was to retain England as a partner in settling international crises, and in particular as a mediator through whose efforts the Balkan situation, once turned to the advantage of the Central Powers by Austrian action against Serbia, could be solidified. In a broader perspective, the success of such limited cooperation might further loosen Anglo-Russian ties, already strained since the autumn of 1912 by tensions over Persia and the Turkish straits and by the Anglo-German mediation of the Balkan wars of 1912–1913. As Riezler recalled for the historian Karl Alexander von Müller in 1915, all of these considerations led Bethmann Hollweg to calculate that, "if the Dual Alliance were again to risk a diplomatic trial of strength, this could only be in Southeastern Europe— that is, where Austria would take the initiative with Germany standing behind it."[5]

In this strategy of calculated risk, the Reich's diplomatic and political maneuverability was threatened from several directions. As Riezler had pointed out, there was the danger both in Germany and elsewhere (especially Russia) that governments following the sober dictates of *raison d'état* could be pushed well beyond their goals by nationalist and expansionist currents. But beyond that—and this was decisive—the operational plans of the general staff for a European war directly contradicted Bethmann Hollweg's political strategy and dangerously limited Germany's options.

The younger Helmuth von Moltke, a nephew of Bismarck's field marshal and chief of the general staff since 1906, held fast to the Schlieffen Plan, revised only in technical detail. It did not call for initial pressure against the Russian "enemy" that, according to the bluff theory, was to be coerced into inaction. Rather, since Moltke envisaged an advance through Belgium, pressure would be brought to bear on the very "partner" whose support was vital for the desired political arrangement, England. And so the solid front of the Entente powers, which the efforts of German diplomacy had loosened somewhat, would be immediately recemented by the deployment of German forces. To be sure, the Reich leadership did attempt to synchronize military planning with political strategy—Foreign Secretary Gottlieb von Jagow proposed an alteration of the operational plan in early 1913—but without success. Thus, unless Germany's enemies renounced the use of force, the lack of cooperation between the political and military realms in Wilhelmine Germany was bound to lead to the dominance of the military at an early stage of the very crisis from which the political leadership, with its conception of "calculated risk," sought to gain an advantage for the Central Powers.

In a memorandum of early 1913 entitled "Germany's Posture in a War of the Triple Alliance," Moltke confirmed the fears of the political leadership that the presence of German troops in Belgium would lead to immediate war with England. But he found himself incapable of returning to his uncle's operational plan, whose strategy for a two-front war was to assume a defensive stance in the west while taking the offensive against Russia. Aside from the real and unheeded foreign policy dangers accompanying a march through Belgium, the course of the First World War showed that Moltke's case for a rapid victory in the west was questionable even from a purely military standpoint. His arguments were based in large part on the fear that the speedier deployment of troops made possible by the expansion of the Russian railway network and the installation of new fortifications would endanger the success of an Austro-German offensive against the Russians in Poland that the elder Moltke had foreseen. "At all events, this Russian campaign would drag on endlessly."[6] Moreover, the organization and deployment planning of the French general staff had improved considerably since the 1870s and 1880s: a strictly defensive stance with reduced troop strength in the west could be maintained only a very short time. French penetration of western Germany, however, would immediately endanger the vital industrial regions of Lorraine, the Saar, and the Ruhr, and lead rapidly to the defeat of the Reich. Finally, Moltke answered the question central to his "west-first" strategy—England's likely response to a German march through Belgium—by openly admitting that, "England too will, and indeed must, side against us, for preventing the Germans from establishing themselves on the channel coast is a matter of life and death to the British. They will never believe that we do not intend that. A German presence on the channel would tie down English sea power there indefinitely and thus render England incapable of maintaining her global position."[7]

Convinced of the inevitability of a great war between the two European blocs, Moltke feared by late 1912 that the German army would be in an "increasingly unfavorable position" due to the broad armaments programs of the other powers: "the enemy was out-arming us."[8] In his statement to the Kaiser on December 8, 1912—"I hold that war is unavoidable, and the sooner the better"[9]—he advocated a specific kind of preventive war. His concept of "preventive war" was not the traditional desire to beat to the punch an enemy preparing for aggression, but was determined by calculations of how the defeat of potential enemies could reverse the adverse flow of events so as to maintain or expand one's own strength.

Between the end of the Balkan crisis in late 1912 and May 1914, Moltke's deliberations on preventive war became considerably more concrete. Speaking to Foreign Secretary von Jagow, he now declared that, in Jagow's words, "the prospects for the future greatly depressed him. In two or three years, Russia will have completed her armaments program. The military superiority of our foes will then be so great that he had no idea how we should overcome them. For the time being, we were still a match for them to some degree. In his opinion, the sole remaining option was to wage preventive war, to strike the enemy while we still had some chance of surviving the struggle."[10]

These then were the preconceptions of the military leadership with which Bethmann Hollweg had to work: an obstinate adherence to the essence of the Schlieffen Plan and a growing tendency toward preventive war. As the Chancellor was powerless to alter them, the chances of success for an active policy based on Riezler's "risk-theory" were slim indeed. The only sensible solution, coupling diplomatic action with military pressure by a political leadership that would use the military as a means to attain its limited political goals, was excluded.

The level of risk was no longer subject to control. It could not be raised, step by step, and then later be reduced. Given the probable expansion of the conflict to include all five great powers and the intensity with which a future war would be waged, the risk would be incalculable. The only remaining ground for hope was that, as Riezler estimated, a political arrangement could be reached following a regional victory because the enormous and clearly perceived risk would itself hinder the outbreak of war. This notion, stated somewhat grimly, still glimmered through in Bethmann Hollweg's remarks during the July crisis. As Riezler noted in his diary, "The Chancellor expects that a war, however it may end, will overturn all that stands."[11]

Either the opposing bloc (and Russia in particular) would shrink before such a prospect, or matters would come to a head —without any intermediate stages—in a great war. In the end, it came down to these alternatives. The weak hope of avoiding a general catastrophe in such a war lay in the chance that fear of creating a revolutionary situation by waging a ruinous, all-out war would lead to an early cessation of the fighting, with the conflict resolved in the style of a limited, eighteenth-century cabinet war. In fact, once Bethmann Hollweg's policies in the July crisis had miscarried, such illusory expectations did guide the political leadership in the first weeks of the war until September 1914.

We may never know what William II meant by his famous comment, "Now or never," written on the June 6, 1914, report from the German Ambassador to Vienna, von Tschirschky, about the Austrian opinion that "there must be a final reckoning with Serbia."[12] But it was decisive for German policy after the assassination at Sarajevo on June 28 that, in a still favorable though rapidly worsening situation, Bethmann Hollweg intended to bring about through an Austrian attack on Serbia the shift in the Balkan balance of power that, in Riezler's theory, could still be accepted by Russia. Presumably, only Russia's prestige and not its vital interests would be affected. The crucial question for Bethmann Hollweg was whether Russia, for reasons of prestige, would perceive support of Serbia as being in her vital interest as a great power. In either case, the choice between peace and general war between the blocs was, in accordance with Riezler's conception, shifted to the enemy. This tied in with the expectation that the German Social Democrats could be persuaded to cooperate in a war in which Russia had thrown down the gauntlet, a defensive war of Germany against "Slavdom."

With the "blank check" given Austria-Hungary on July 5–6, Bethmann Hollweg inaugurated his policy of calculated risk. Through rapid action against Serbia, Bethmann Hollweg hoped to capitalize on Russia's presumed sense of monarchical solidarity, which, it was hoped, would paralyze her policy following the murder of the Habsburg heir. Austria-Hungary's position as a great power would thus be enhanced in two ways: first, by creating a *fait accompli,* and then, in concert with the Entente, by bringing about a settlement to the crisis. In Riezler's shorthand, "a *fait accompli,* and then friendly toward the Entente, and the shock can be absorbed."[13]

But the German side overlooked the fact that—quite apart from the Dual Monarchy's dubious military capacity—agreement between the representatives of the Hungarian and Austrian halves of the empire first had to be reached in foreign policy as in all major decisions. This was as a rule a painfully slow process, and in this case, Hungary did not have the slightest interest in expanding at Serbia's expense nor, especially, in including new Slavic territories in the Empire. Thus, on the Austro-Hungarian side, the crucial political and military prerequisites were lacking for the surprise attack on Serbia that the Germans expected.

Bethmann Hollweg thought from the beginning that his approach had only a slight chance of success, which would diminish the longer Austria-Hungary delayed. In his opinion, "Whoever considers that Russia could never stand to be crossed in the Balkans," and concludes that Germany "therefore ought not support Austria-Hungary in her move against Serbia, imputes German self-emasculation."[14] The decline of the Danubian monarchy would, to the Chancellor's mind, then be unavoidable and would bring the Reich itself into hopeless dependence upon Russia. As Bethmann Hollweg later defended his actions during the July crisis in his memoirs, such a capitulation would have been intolerable. His retrospective account, while camouflaging the active German role in pressing Austria-Hungary's action against Serbia, confirms the alternatives that the Chancellor believed he faced on July 5 and 6: either exploit the opportunity, scant though it now was, and take the related risk, or capitulate to the general trend of European developments that threatened to lead Germany, with the loss of its last ally, into complete isolation.

By the onset of the July crisis, Bethmann Hollweg had no illusions about the great risk of war. He knew that it was "hardly possible" that Austria-Hungary could be "led by the hand from Berlin,"[15] by first inducing it to strike suddenly against Serbia and then bringing it to the negotiating table before the other great powers had, in Riezler's terms, "bluffed" themselves to the point of no return.[16] The Chancellor noted pessimistically on July 7 that "action against Serbia can lead to world war,"[17] and on July 8 that "if war does not come, if the czar does not want it or if a startled France counsels peace, then we will still have a chance to split the Entente."[18]

For Bethmann Hollweg, a whole range of reasons compelled him to seize upon the slight chance that remained. As he explained to Riezler immediately following his decision on the evening of July 6, "The Entente knows that Germany is 'absolutely paralyzed.' Austria is becoming ever weaker and less mobile. Russia's military strength is growing rapidly. The secret reports of Anglo-Russian naval discussions indicate the serious possibility of an English attempt to land forces in Pomerania in case of war." If Germany failed to provide support, "then Austria-Hungary will approach the Western powers, whose arms are open, and we will lose our last military ally."[19]

What was decisive for Bethmann Hollweg was Russia's steadily "growing presumptions and her enormous force for disruption." "The future [belongs] to Russia, which grows and grows and grows, and which hangs over us like an increasingly horrible incubus." "In a few years there will be no defense against it, particularly if the present European alignments [persist]."[20] In testimony before the Investigating Committee of the German National Assembly in 1919, Bethmann Hollweg judged that "to retreat from the position to which, despite the constant risk of war, we had previously adhered and abandon Austria-Hungary would have meant the demolition of our own global position without a struggle."[21]

It soon became obvious that Austria-Hungary was unable to move quickly against Serbia, so that advantages were lost that might have favored success in the period directly after the Sarajevo murder. The Chancellor stood by his initial decision, however, because he now more than ever saw "capitulation" as the sole alternative. On July 18, Foreign Secretary von Jagow outlined the goals of the Reich leadership for the German ambassador in London, Prince Lichnowsky, as follows:

> We must see to it that the conflict between Austria and Serbia is localized. Whether or not this succeeds depends first on Russia and second on the restraining influence of her Entente partners. The more determined Austria appears and the more energetically we support it, the more readily Russia will keep still . . . France and England also do not want war now. According to all competent analyses, Russia will be ready for war in a few years. Then the number of its soldiers will crush us; then it will have completed construction of its Baltic fleet and strategic railways. In the meantime, our group will grow ever weaker. The Russians are well aware of this, and therefore desire nothing but peace and quiet for a few more years . . . If the conflict cannot be localized, and Russia attacks Austria, then that is our *causus foederis*. At that point, we cannot abandon Austria. For we would then stand in an isolation that could hardly be called proud. I do not want a preventive war, but if war there will be, we cannot shirk it.[22]

Three days earlier, Jagow had written privately to shipping magnate Albert Ballin: "The feeling that the iron ring surrounding us will keep tightening might, in view of the threats from Russia's growing strength and an increasingly aggressive Pan-Slavism, sooner or later lead to dangerous consequences."[23] These statements show the extent to which the civilian leadership had come to share the outlook of the chief of the general staff, Moltke. The most important points of accord between the political leadership and the general staff concerned the steadily increasing Russian threat and the assumption, by now axiomatic, that in a few years Germany would be brought to its knees in a politically and strategically hopeless position without a drop of blood being shed. In his discussion with Jagow in late May 1914, Moltke had tried to enlist the Foreign Secretary's support for "our policy of quickly bringing about a war."[24] At that time, Jagow had responded that he could "not agree with . . . conjuring up a preventive war—quite aside from the fact that the appropriate moment for it had perhaps already been missed [when the Triple Entente was forged, or in 1908–1909, when Russia was still notoriously ill-prepared for war]." Jagow still hoped that "it would be possible to improve our relationship with England to the point that general war would be pretty much out of the question, or at least less of a threat. For without England's backing, Russia and France would hardly risk provoking armed conflict with us. But Germany, if its economic position were allowed to develop peacefully, would automatically grow ever stronger and more difficult to vanquish."[25]

Looking back in 1919, Jagow noted that he had hoped to the very end "that a general war could be avoided." "But I cannot deny that [when] this proved impossible, the memory of Moltke's remarks of late May 1914 that 'there was nothing left but to wage a preventive war while we could still withstand it so some degree' gave me a measure of confidence in a positive outcome."[26] In other words, the political leadership knowingly ran such a great risk in the July crisis because it was convinced that should the other side choose war, the odds for military victory by the Central Powers were better than they would be several years hence. For the political leadership the crisis thus became the "touchstone of whether Russia too would not shrink from employing force in pursuit of its interests now that it was more powerful than in previous crises and from letting it come to war if need be. If the Russians showed themselves ready for war now, that was all the more reason to expect a similar resolve in coming years, when the alliance system would be subject to crises and power-probes under circumstances less favorable to Germany."[27]

This was why Bethmann Hollweg considered that any English mediation before the first tangible successes of the attack against Serbia would be premature. Despite all warnings, he continued to insist that the attack against an isolated Serbia had to take place. He expected the Austrian march to the south to be carried out in full, even though this would entail enormous difficulties in case of a general war, serving to detour Austrian forces against Russia and compromise Austria's ability to fulfill the vaguely stated agreements for the coalition's waging of the war. (Soon, this would in fact seriously burden the Austro-German partnership.)

Only on July 24, the second day of the Austro-Serbian war—following Austria's first engagement against Serbia (the bombardment of Belgrade) and the unsettling reports of Russian military preparations—did Bethmann Hollweg conclude that the moment had come to reduce the crisis and to move toward the diplomatic mediation England urged. England seemed to see the temporary Austrian occupation of the area around Belgrade as the basis for a settlement.

Now everything depended upon how the czar would react. German hopes that Russia would accept the Austrian action "with a few rumbling noises"[28] were based on the knowledge that the Russian army was not yet ready for war. If Russian War Minister Sukhomlinov (like his predecessor Roediger in 1909) admitted to the czar the army's true weakness, then the Russian government would have to accept a new and heavy diplomatic defeat. But in the decisive privy council meeting at Krasnoselye on July 25, Sukhomlinov did not issue the warning that it was his duty to give. Instead he thought it best to "show personal courage" by remaining silent; in the process he "seriously deluded himself concerning the capacity of the army he had reorganized."[29] And so the decision was made to begin military preparations to meet the Austro-Hungarian invasion of Serbia with armed force. Preliminary mobilization was first thought of as a means of pressuring Austria-Hungary to hold back in Serbia and thus give up its plan of a localized war. By July 29 at the latest, however, Russia had come to expect war. For Foreign Minister Sazanov, the strongest personality in Saint Petersburg, the argument that Russia's prestige as a great power had to be upheld by aiding Serbia was decisive in the resolution for war.

On the German side, meanwhile, Bethmann Hollweg had already begun to despair of a rational management of the crisis. On July 26 he again outlined the basic thrust of his policy, urging that Germany do nothing that could be interpreted in Russia as showing preparedness for or, worse, intent of war. From anti-Serbian demonstrations on the return of the Kaiser from his

Scandinavian journey, Russia "would conclude that we want war. This would be premature so long as Russia takes no aggressive steps whatsoever. But whatever ensues Russia must relentlessly be placed in the wrong."[30] On July 27, the eve of the Austrian declaration of war against Serbia engineered by Bethmann Hollweg, Riezler summed up his impression of the Chancellor's attitude: "The Chancellor sees a Fate, greater than human power, lying over the situation in Europe and over our people."[31] Yet Bethmann Hollweg still believed on July 28 that the change of course toward a diminution of the crisis ("Stop in Belgrade"[32]) sought by the Kaiser and a turn to diplomatic mediation were premature—even though a compromise solution on the basis proposed by William II could likely have been found, at least with England. But that would have meant renouncing the larger regional success that Bethmann Hollweg sought.

Only on the following day did a more grave estimate of the situation lead the government to hastily attempt to brake the momentum of the crisis and steer it toward a political arrangement based upon gains achieved. By now, however, Bethmann Hollweg's ability to negotiate had shrunk to a minimum: on that same day the first reports of Russian mobilization arrived. As was to be expected in view of the time-dependent operational planning of the German general staff, this news gave military policy precedence over Bethmann Hollweg's political strategy. That strategy, because of the military build-up in the west—in effect directed also against England—now lost its underpinnings. German diplomacy was thus reduced to the servile role of shielding military planning.

Also contributing to the collapse of the Chancellor's political strategy was his inability to induce Vienna to suddenly break off the attack just begun against Serbia and accept British mediation that the German government itself had heretofore shunned. Bethmann Hollweg had always seen this shift as a truly critical moment in his calculations, but now it had become, with lightning speed, of overwhelming importance. The Austro-Hungarian regime, however, having once made up its mind to crush Serbia for the sake of its own prestige as a great power, was firm in its resolve to carry out this limited undertaking, indeed without regard for the threat of a general war. Vienna was not to be dissuaded by the belated diplomatic maneuvers of its German ally.

Bethmann Hollweg therefore had to acknowledge at the meeting of the Prussian Ministry of State on July 30, that although "all governments—including Russia's—and the great majority of peoples were, in and of themselves, peaceable, we have lost control and the stone has begun to roll."[33] The great European war, in which, thanks to German military planning, all five great powers took part from the beginning, could no longer be limited by the desperate maneuvers of German diplomacy, itself now fully in the service of military strategy. The attempt to rationally manage the crisis had yielded to the "leap into the dark" of which Bethmann Hollweg had spoken as early as July 14.[34]

The German military plan, on which the future of the Reich and its ally now depended, was, however, linked to so many improbabilities (hence the expression "leap into the dark") that a totally favorable outcome was not to be expected. First, France had to be defeated in the shortest possible time. Moltke, in his last conversation with his Austrian counterpart, General Conrad von Hötzendorf, in May 1914, had given it six weeks (thus correcting earlier estimates of three to five weeks). Second, the plan called for victory over Russia by late autumn of the same year. Finally, England would then have to come to terms with the situation created by the German triumph in continental Europe and declare itself ready for some form of compromise with the new hegemonic power.

Together with Schlieffen's plan, Moltke had taken up—though without real conviction—his maxim that Germany had to aim for a short war because of its economic vulnerability. Discussions of economic preparations for war had taken place between various departments (general staff, Prussian War Ministry, Reich Interior Ministry) since the autumn of 1912. But the results were insignificant; the civilian agencies did not comply sufficiently with the military's demands concerning economic provisions in case of war. The level of Germany's economic mobilization on the eve of war therefore fell well behind the goals set by the military. And even if the political agencies had been more prudent, the division between state and economy that

marked the liberal system would have allowed for no bold planning of the economy for wartime.

In January 1914 the Reich still had two basic choices in economic policy: to alter fundamentally the economic course by
concentrating German foreign trade in continental Europe
(urged as early as 1912 by the influential president of the Allge-
meine-Elektrizitäts-Gesellschaft, Walter Rathenau) or to stay
with the worldwide orientation of German foreign trade policy.
The leadership opted for the policy on which the great rise of
German industry had been founded, continued orientation
toward the world market. In late August, after the outbreak of
the war, American ambassador Gerard addressed the economic
question in a discussion with Deutsche Bank director Gwinner:
"In another twenty-five years, no one could have stood up to
[the Germans] the way they were developing. Now [they] have
wagered everything on a single card. [I don't] understand how
the Kaiser could have decided to do this."[35] The Hamburg
banker Max Warburg concurred. A week before the Sarajevo
assassination Warburg replied to the Kaiser's remark that Russia's armaments indicated her intention to start a war in 1916:
"Germany is growing stronger with every year of peace. Waiting
can only bring us rewards."[36]

In fact, the decision for war cannot be understood in economic terms. Even if one exaggerates the peacetime feasibility of
Rathenau's alternative of a relatively closed, German-led "Middle European" economic area, the fact remains that from a realistic economic viewpoint the expected gains in Europe would be
no match for unavoidable losses throughout the world. This
would certainly be true in the British Empire, which was the
largest market for German exports, and very likely in South
America and East Asia as well. One can only comprehend the
resolve for war in terms of Wilhelmine Germany's understanding of what it meant to be a great power. Military and strategic
considerations were singularly important, while other factors,
including the economic, were denied equal weight in the leadership's analysis of Germany's situation.

The German government's decision for war in late July 1914
was a consequence of the collision between Russian and Austro-
German political offensives, each with the goal of organizing the

Balkan countries under its own leadership. With the decision to force a resolution in favor of the Central Powers by means of a localized war against Serbia, the Reich leadership consciously risked a greater war. That war became a certainty as Russia confounded German expectations that its military weakness would lead it to accept the defeat of its Balkan policy and instead, following the Austrian invasion of Serbia, made preparations for war. All this ran counter to Bethmann Hollweg's calculations. But for Germany to yield in these altered circumstances—given the great powers' mania for prestige in that period, and particularly the German obsession with the military aspects of power— would have been tantamount to capitulation.

Bethmann Hollweg's concept of calculated risk in the July crisis of 1914 was dubious from the start. Today it appears almost archaic, though in many characteristics it seems to anticipate present-day political-strategic calculations. Even if (unlike Fritz Fischer in *Germany's Aims in the First World War*) one is unable to recognize any desire by the political leadership for far-reaching expansion in 1914, but considers the conduct of Bethmann Hollweg in making the critical decisions of July 5–6 and 28–29 as determined by a political strategy of limited objectives, the German government's share of responsibility for the outbreak of the Great War is nevertheless evident. After unsuccessful and not particularly forceful attempts to dissuade Austria-Hungary at the last hour, the civilian leadership recognized the failure of its political strategy and so opened the way for the preventive war urged by the military.

Bethmann Hollweg acknowledged this shared guilt. He told the journalist Theodor Wolff on February 5, 1915: "When one discusses the responsibility for this war, we must honestly recognize that we too deserve our share of the blame. It would be an understatement to say that this thought oppresses me. The thought does not leave me. I live in it."[37] After the fall of this first and most important war chancellor in July 1917, Reichstag member Conrad Haussmann wrote of his meeting with Bethmann Hollweg, then living in retirement at Hohenfinow: "A monstrous pressure is still upon him . . . because he carries with him Germany's guilt or joint responsibility for the war." The former chancellor himself admitted to Haussmann: "This war rages inside me. I continually ask myself if it could have been avoided, what I could have done. All nations bear responsibility for it; Germany too shares a great part of the blame . . . In a certain sense it was a preventive war. But when war was hanging over us, when in two years it would have been even more dangerous and inescapable, and when the military says, 'now it is still possible without being defeated, but not in two years!' . . . "[38]

4

NEW GERMAN
FOREIGN POLICY OBJECTIVES,
1914–1918

I N contemporary historical discussion there are two opposing interpretations of German foreign policy aims from the Wilhelmine era to Hitler. One thesis, most forcefully represented by Fritz Fischer, argues for the unbroken continuity of imperialistic goals from the era of William II, through the First World War, and through the period of the Weimar Republic down to Hitler's brazen attempt to establish Germany as a world power. Another interpretation, long dominant in West Germany and still widespread, argues that there is no connection between the German war goals in the first and second world wars. Neither of these is convincing. On the one hand, continuities certainly exist, while on the other hand deep breaches and important new departures can be identified. Despite the partial truth of each position, there are compelling reasons for a third interpretation: that a far-reaching change took place *during* the First World War. Earlier objectives were displaced by related but qualitatively different aims often approaching Hitler's later program without, however, bearing his decisive stamp. The origin of the Second World War, or to be more precise, the history of Germany's role in the coming of the second Great War, begins with the First World War. Here lie important roots of Hitler's radical and far-ranging program.

It would be an all too easy solution to the oft-mentioned problem of the caesura in German history during the First

World War to see the swearing-in of the Third Army Command under Field Marshal Paul von Hindenburg and the real leader, General Erich von Ludendorff, in August 1916 as the only critical turning point among ongoing changes of leadership and goals. Similarly, one cannot view the following period (at the latest after Bethmann Hollweg's fall in July 1917) solely in terms of Ludendorff's quasi-dictatorship. It is clear, however, that Bethmann Hollweg, the leading proponent in government of sharply delineated war aims, was first outmaneuvered and finally fired by the stronger supporters of the new policies. To be sure, the new Foreign Secretary, Richard von Kühlmann—in near isolation within the leadership—sought to carry on Bethmann Hollweg's policies until his own dismissal in July 1918. Only then did Bethmann Hollweg's old line, now hardly recognizable, finally disappear.

Thus the field was left entirely to the opposition, the Third Army Command dominated by Ludendorff. It could regard itself as representing a movement that had grown ever stronger within the leadership and among the general public in the first three years of the unexpectedly long and difficult war, and it grew by leaps and bounds in 1918. Leaders of this movement perceived the war's objectives as fundamentally different from those transitional ones identified with Bethmann Hollweg's so-called September Program of 1914. In the short optimistic period before the battle of the Marne (September 14, 1914), the Chancellor had called for the "securing of the German Reich in both east and west for the indefinite future."[1]

The basic differences between these positions can best be understood by contrasting two revealing statements by Bethmann Hollweg and Ludendorff to see how each defined a German victory. After the failure of German strategy in the battle of the Marne, General Erich von Falkenhayn, Moltke's successor as chief of the general staff, admitted on November 18 that Germany could not defeat the Triple Entente. Bethmann Hollweg's subsequent policy recognized that if Germany showed the world that it could not be conquered, that its potential for growth could not be arrested, and that it could successfully defend the accomplishments of 1870, then "we should be thankful to God."[2] That is to say, if the Reich survived this struggle for "self-preservation" without losses of territory or power it had already won, Germany would have proved that it could not be overpowered by the strongest coalition in Europe. Ludendorff, on the other hand, believed that "a peace which only guarantees the territorial status quo would mean that we had lost the war."[3]

To avoid misunderstanding it must be added that Bethmann Hollweg's goal of a peace based on German "self-preservation" did not exclude an extension of German power, either by annexations or the indirect device of "guarantees and securities" in both east and west, should the enemy declare such terms acceptable at a military juncture favorable to the Central Powers. But territorial gains or any other form of German aggrandizement were not, to Bethmann Hollweg, sufficient reasons for continuing the war if the enemy were prepared to accept a peace on the basis of the *status quo ante*.

Behind these old and new sets of war goals—which in fact seldom conflicted so long as the leadership did not face a concrete decision on the question of peace—there were differing conceptions of the meaning of great power status. Bethmann Hollweg, and later Kühlmann, strove for the maintenance or restoration, and if possible, improvement, of Germany's great power position. They did so in the traditional manner, seeking to secure both freedom of action in foreign policy and the capacity to forge military alliances within the confines of a European state system based upon the principle of peace as the norm. Opposing this was the "modern" conception of great power status advanced by Ludendorff and other strong forces in the leadership. Their viewpoint presumed that a permanent state of war —interrupted only by cease-fires—existed between those European great powers contending for positions of world power. Accordingly, the only powers that stood a chance of surviving the expected *next* world war would be those that emerged from the present one with greatly expanded territory and power. From this perspective, a return to the pre-1914 status quo would mean a step backward that could only lead the affected power sooner or later to insignificance in world politics.

Kühlmann's statement in the spring of 1918 that, "what was determined and signed at Brest-Litovsk is to be seen as only provisional, pending a general peace settlement,"[4] was perhaps the last gasp of the old policy, now almost robbed of meaning by the dominant influence of the Third Army Command. One sign of just how isolated the Foreign Secretary's interpretation of the German-Soviet Treaty of Brest-Litovsk (March 3, 1918) was, how restricted his room for negotiation, how slight the possibility of realizing a policy of reason and compromise, and how steadily his domestic opposition had gained in strength, was Ludendorff's agreement to circulate the war aims of the Pan-German League that had been suppressed by Bethmann Hollweg in December 1914. The League called for driving Russia back to the borders that Peter the Great had inherited and consolidating the widely scattered German elements in Russia, annexing Belgium and northeastern France, and turning Toulon into a German port on the Mediterranean—to cite only the most important demands. These demands were now circulated in 35,000 pamphlets. Reflecting its successful propaganda and its proximity to official policy, the Pan-German League's membership rose to its highest level. The German Fatherland Party, a more widely based indicator of the strength behind the Third Army Command and its goals, counted 1.25 million members in July 1918 and thus surpassed the heretofore largest party, the Social Democrats (SPD), in membership if not in potential voting strength.

The new war aims were most clearly evident in Germany's eastern policy of 1918. The prospect of being able—directly or indirectly—to control and economically exploit not only the western border zones but all of Russia as well left far behind all earlier plans to forge the political and economic energies of Central Europe into a German-led union. The idea of a "Middle Europe," oriented toward the new hegemonic power, Germany, had undergone a variety of redefinitions since September 1914. In its place there now emerged the new goal: the creation of an eastern sphere ruled by Germany alone.

Such a conception represented a third and final phase in the development of political and economic goals in the Wilhelmine era. Before August 1914, adherents of a world-market orientation had largely determined official policy. With the severing of Germany's links to global markets by the British blockade, however, exponents of an economic and foreign trade policy concentrating on "Middle Europe" won the day, thus introducing the second phase. The Middle Europe idea, from its first outlines in Bethmann Hollweg's September Memorandum in 1914 moved increasingly—largely because of Entente threats to wage economic war against the Central Powers after the end of the military conflict—in the direction of total separation and economic self-sufficiency in the form of an economic union of associated nations under German leadership. The greatest weakness of the concept, in terms of realizing Germany's absolute potential, was continued German dependence on other sovereign states. The possibility, which leaped to the fore in the spring of 1918, of winning the entire, expansive eastern sphere [*Ostraum*] with its supposedly inexhaustible supplies of raw materials as a "German hinterland" had no such limitation.

Germany's grandiose plans for the East, growing out of nearly four years of war, involved a concept of autarky that was linked to securing the Reich strategically on a vast front with a future war in mind. Control over a broad and, so far as possible, self-enclosed territory, conceived on a continental order of magnitude, came to be seen as an absolute necessity because of the rapid wartime development of a military technology capable of overrunning ever vaster areas. A "Middle European" Reich, surrounded by potential enemies, limited to relatively narrow confines, with vulnerable industrial centers near its borders, could —so ran the logic of this argument—be indirectly held at bay militarily and strategically even without a new war. To escape this development, the goal of the present war had been winning a self-contained and truly defensible sphere of control.

A basic axiom of the 1918 eastern policy held that it was entirely possible for Germany to take all of Russia in its grasp and keep the giant empire in an enduring state of dependency. This was perhaps the most significant addition to German considerations of power politics since it had the longest after-effect. It stood in direct contradiction to the exaggerated estimates of Russian strength that had so distressed both government and military in the years before 1914. Bethmann Hollweg had been haunted by the nightmare that Russia would some day realize her seemingly limitless potential by crushing the Central Powers. But following the devastating defeats suffered by the Russian

army in 1914–1915 and the open outbreak of national and social tensions within the czarist empire (which the Germans
imagined their "psychological warfare" to have promoted in
good part), perceptions of overwhelming Russian strength gave
way to expectations of continued weakness, at least for the near
future. A new-style German power politics aimed to exploit this
weakness.

In the first years of the war, the idea—articulated as early as
1914—of constructing a German "security cordon" in Poland
and the Baltic nations presupposed that Russia would quickly
recover after the war. Insofar as possible, then, a barrier had to
be erected. Yet until the autumn of 1916 even this objective remained subordinate to the hope of concluding a separate peace
with the czar, essentially on the basis of the *status quo ante* with
only a slight strip of the Polish border to be retained by Germany. After the Russian Revolution of 1917, however, a different point of view—already espoused by several leading publi-
cists in the prewar period—won the upper hand. The Russian
empire was deemed unstable enough that it could, with some
skillful help from the outside, be broken apart.

The *völkisch* settlement and colonization plans that were then
proposed for the vast eastern sphere were themselves not new.
The permeation of Social Darwinist ideas, even among German
officialdom, had begun well before 1914. It proceeded apace
after the war's outbreak and drove the government, even under
Bethmann Hollweg, to make concessions. Only in 1918, however, with the final triumph of the forces represented by the
Third Army Command, did these ideas fully dominate the highest leadership of the Reich.

To understand later German history one must pay special attention to a consequence of the eastern situation in the autumn
of 1918 that has often been overlooked: the widely shared and
strangely irrational misconceptions concerning the end of the
war that found such currency in the Weimar period. These ideas
were not informed, as they should have been, by an appreciation
of the enemy's superiority in the west and the inevitable step-by-
step retreat of the German western front before the massive in-
flux of Americans. Nor did they indicate any understanding of
the catastrophic consequences for the Central Powers following

the collapse of the Balkan front after Bulgaria's withdrawal from the war. They were instead largely determined by the fact that German troops, as "victors," held vast strategically and economically important areas of Russia.

At the moment of the November 1918 ceasefire in the west, newspaper maps of the military situation showed German troops in Finland, holding the line from the Finnish fjords near Narva, down through Pskov-Orsha-Mogilev and the area south of Kursk, to the Don east of Rostov. Germany had thus secured the Ukraine. The Russian recognition of the Ukraine's separation exacted at Brest-Litovsk represented the key element in German efforts to keep Russia perpetually subservient. In addition, German troops held the Crimea and were stationed in smaller numbers in Transcaucasia. Even the unoccupied "rump-Russia" appeared—with the conclusion of the German-Soviet Supplementary Treaty on August 28, 1918—to be in firm though indirect dependency on the Reich. Thus, Hitler's long-range aim, fixed in the 1920s, of erecting a German Eastern Imperium on the ruins of the Soviet Union was not simply a vision emanating from an abstract wish. In the eastern sphere established in 1918, this goal had a concrete point of departure. The German Eastern Imperium had already been—if only for a short time—a reality.

But the most important factor impeding a realistic postwar foreign policy grew out of a decisive failure on the part of the government under Bethmann Hollweg. Its domestic policies did not concur with a need clearly recognized after November 18, 1914: to end the war as quickly as possible on tolerable terms, since a German victory over the Triple Entente was now out of the question. Above all, it would have been necessary to lead the German public gradually toward a realistic assessment of the Reich's position in the war and to an appreciation of what could at best still be achieved, the maintenance of the status quo.

Instead, the rising expectation of victory in the years before 1917 and especially in the period of partial military dictatorship (1917–1918), during an undreamed-of show of German national strength, had to be suddenly shattered in the fall of 1918. But the illusion did not die with military defeat. The false assessment of Germany's relative power, which began far back in the

Wilhelmine years of peace, was fatefully inflated because of its seeming confirmation during the war as the German army resisted "a world of enemies." Against such illusions the Reich leadership under Bethmann Hollweg, which certainly knew better, and the later governments of the Weimar Republic were helpless.

"World power or decline"—these were the alternatives posed by Friedrich von Bernhardi in his enormously popular book *Germany and the Next War* (1912) as the consequences of a coming struggle between the European powers. Although the issue was resolved in 1918 to Germany's disadvantage, Hitler carried it to a new extreme with his pronouncement, "Germany will either be a world power, or there will be no Germany,"[5] and worked it into a specific program. In this form it found such strong adherence that the wave of irrational aspirations that carried him along and that he encouraged drowned the Weimar attempt to institute a soberly conceived German foreign policy of moderation.

5
HITLER'S PROGRAM

H ITLER's conception of his future foreign policy developed
in many stages between 1919 and 1928 before solidi-
fying into a firm program, to which he then single-mindedly adhered until his suicide in the Reich Chancellery on April 30,
1945. What was at once decisive and totally novel in the formation of his program—and this must be stressed—was the complete permeation of originally crude Machiavellian objectives by
the most radical variety of anti-Semitism. Although he drew on
the theory of the worldwide Jewish conspiracy as propagated in
the "Protocols of the Elders of Zion," widely distributed by
White Russian immigrants in *völkisch* circles in Germany in
1919–1920, there were, in Hitler's case, crucial psychological
factors.[1] The wide-ranging political aims of Hitler's foreign policy were subordinated to a central goal: the eradication of the
Jewish "archenemy."

The full scope and thrust of the foreign policy which Hitler
had already set as his life's mission in the 1920s became clear
only some time after the Second World War with the enrich-
ment of our source materials, especially through the publication
of Hitler's early speeches and his "Second Book" of 1928.[2] This
documentation made it possible to place the programmatic ut-
terances of *Mein Kampf,* which previously had appeared frag-
mentary and unrelated to the actual practice of the Third Reich
(at least in the years of peace) in the context of their origin and

49

elaboration. In time it became clear how systematically Hitler had pursued his aims after the mid-1920s without, however, forfeiting any of his tactical flexibility. It emerged that the sentence printed in bold-face letters in *Mein Kampf,* "Germany will either be a world power or there will be no Germany," was, quite literally, the crux of Hitler's program.

In brief, his aim was this. After gaining power in Germany and consolidating his rule in Central Europe, he would lead the Reich to a position of world power in two main stages. First, he would set up a continental empire that would control all Europe with a solid economic and strategic power base in vast stretches of Eastern Europe. Then, by adding a colonial realm in Africa and by building a strong Atlantic-based navy, he would make Germany one of the four remaining world powers (after forcing out France and Russia), beside the British Empire, the Japanese sphere in East Asia, and (most important to Hitler's mind) the United States. He anticipated for the generation after his death a decisive struggle between the two leading world powers, Germany and America, for a sort of world dominion. For this violent confrontation in the future, a battle of continents, he wanted to create in his own time the necessary geopolitical basis (the "sphere of control") for the anticipated "Germanic Empire of the German Nation." Failing this, as Hitler saw the alternative, Germany would inevitably be condemned to insignificance in world politics.

In his "Second Book," Hitler rated American strength extremely high, albeit assuming that it would reach its apogee only around 1980. He therefore saw the unification of all Europe under his rule as imperative, and an alliance between this super-Germany and the British Empire as desirable in order to challenge America later.[3] By contrast, he held Russian power in extraordinarily low esteem. He believed that a Germany shaped by racial principles need not fear a potential Russian world power, as they should fear the racially "high-grade" Americans. "These people," he wrote of the Russians at a crucial juncture in his "Second Book,"

> live in a state structure whose value, judged traditionally, would have to be even higher than that of the United States. Despite this, however, it would never occur to anybody to fear Russian

world hegemony for this reason. No such inner value is attached to the number of Russian people that this number could endanger the freedom of the world. At least never [like the United States] in the sense of an economic and political mastery of other parts of the globe, but at most in the sense of an inundation by disease bacilli which at the moment have their breeding ground in Russia.[4]

The conquest of European Russia, the cornerstone of the continental European phase of his program, was thus for Hitler inextricably linked with the extermination of these "bacilli," the Jews. In his conception they had gained dominance over Russia with the Bolshevik Revolution. Russia thereby became the center from which a global danger radiated, particularly threatening to the Aryan race and its German core. To Hitler, Bolshevism meant the consummate rule of Jewry, while democracy —as it had developed in Western Europe and Weimar Germany —represented a preliminary stage of Bolshevism, since the Jews had there won a leading, if not yet a dominant influence. This racist component of Hitler's thought was so closely interwoven with the central political element of his program, the conquest of European Russia, that Russia's defeat and the extermination of the Jews were—in theory as later in practice—inseparable for him. To the aim of expansion per se, however, Hitler gave not racial but political, strategic, economic, and demographic underpinnings.

By what method was he to reach this goal, so fantastic from the standpoint of 1928, but brought so close to realization in the turbulent years from the beginning of 1938 to the end of 1941? To understand Hitler's method one must assume that in the development of his schemes, as later in their execution, he had already come to terms, in a complex manner, with the real and imagined experiences of the First World War. Together with his prewar Vienna period and postwar Munich years, the war provided the politician (and later commander-in-chief) Hitler with his formative experiences. It made him recognize the impossibility of a German victory in a war where Germany was pitted against both the continental power, Russia, and the British Empire, let alone the two Anglo-Saxon sea powers. His memory was alive with the hopelessness of Germany's predicament surrounded by enemies in a Central European bastion—even one somewhat expanded by larger perimeters in east and west—in a world war in which the superior economic and armaments potential of the hostile coalition would ultimately tell. While holding firmly to Ludendorff's expansive principles of the latter phase of the First World War,[5] Hitler linked these to considerations of power politics and geopolitical perspectives and drew his own unique conclusions.

In following a systematic foreign policy whose final prize was to be reached in several stages, the immediate objective had always to be limited to a single direction of expansion. The net gain of these intermediate goals (seen in both military-economic and strategic terms, with an eye to the great war expected in the future) was to bring Germany into such a favorable situation that a repetition of the Reich's predicament in the First World War would be forever excluded. The basic hypothesis of the politically and ideologically decisive phase of this program, Germany's "break out" to the east, was that Germany would defer colonial and overseas ambitions in return for British recognition of German hegemony over continental Europe (including European Russia), with the United States standing aside. With his typical equation of political with territorial interests in all great power politics (which he understood in terms of "spheres of influence"), Hitler was incapable of foreseeing any conflict with British and American interests in this phase of his program for expansion. "England does not want Germany to be a world power; but France wants no power that is named Germany," he had maintained in *Mein Kampf.* "Today, however"—that is, the period of the Weimar Republic in the mid-1920s—"we are not fighting for a world power position."[6] Thus, for this period of struggle "for the survival of the Fatherland" (as also for the following period of German expansion on the continent) he deemed an alliance with Great Britain possible and desirable. Furthermore—and this is crucial to an understanding of Hitler's practice of foreign policy from 1933 to 1941—the alliance was to take the form of a "grand solution" involving German dominance over the whole of continental Europe.

Hitler's ultimate aspiration in power politics, however, went well beyond this. To his mind, the achievement of German rule over continental Europe would itself provide the basis for a German position of world power. This position would then, in a new phase of imperialist expansion—with a view toward an ultimate war with America—be built by a strong German navy and a large colonial empire in Africa. If possible, this would be accomplished with England's acquiescence and at the expense of France, which was to be defeated before the conquest of the East.

The preliminary stage of the program, the winning of a broader base in Central Europe, was to be reached by gradual expansion of German territory and initially by peaceful means. Here the slogan "struggle against Versailles" and the exploitation of pan-German agitation in German Austria and the Habsburg successor-states provided the best opportunities to conceal the real, far more extensive aims. When these means had been exhausted, further partial objectives would be won through localized wars, using a qualitatively superior army against one enemy at a time. In addition to the political gains, Germany's meager military-economic base would thus be broadened to such an extent that the German-ruled sphere could withstand a new world war even with a comprehensive economic blockade by the sea powers. But until that time Germany's position would be vulnerable and a great, long war was to be avoided at all costs.

Only when all of these steps had been taken would Germany no longer need fear the quantitative arms and economic superiority of the established world powers, including American potential. Germany's military-economic and geographical base area, an armaments program geared to superior quality, not quantity, and Hitler's conception of "lightning war" (*Blitzkrieg*) were all closely related central components of his method. If despite such obviously difficult preconditions all the premises proved valid, Hitler believed that he would succeed in creating an autarkic, blockade-proof, and defensible sphere that would grant Germany real autonomy (and not just formal sovereignty) for all time. In short, he would create a German world power to stand beside the other world powers.

In comparison with the German war goals developed during the First World War, Hitler's aims were radically simplified;

moreover, the racial-ideological conclusions drawn in his program, which were directed to a complete transformation of Europe along racial principles, represented something entirely different. True, purely in terms of power politics and territory, the war goals of the latter part of the war were not so different from Nazi expansionist aims. But to Hitler, the prerequisite for the establishment and maintenance of German rule over Europe was the physical extermination of the Russian ruling stratum and its putative basis, the millions of Eastern European Jews. In National Socialist ideology, this prerequisite was grounded in the mythical link between Bolshevist rule and Jewry. It was to be followed by the destruction of all Jews in the rest of continental Europe, subjugated, directly or indirectly, to German control. The diverse territories of the former Russian state were not merely, like the rest of continental Europe, to be brought into close dependence on Germany, but reduced to the level of colonies, to be exploited economically and settled by members of the ruling race. Colonialism, which in the imperialist era had been limited to overseas regions and suggestions of which had marked Germany's eastern policy in 1918 (and to a lesser extent the later Allied intervention in the Soviet Union), was now fully transferred to Europe.

These enormous schemes, and particularly their connection with racist ideology, were, to be sure, the program of a single individual. But in the case of such prominent provisions as the revision of the Versailles Treaty and the creation of a "Greater Germany," they overlapped with the aims of the old German leadership and the fantasies of a large part of the German public that had never assimilated the loss of the war. To this one must add, however, that the essence of Hitler's program "violated all traditions of German foreign policy and foresook all established standards and concepts to such a radical degree that it . . . did not penetrate the consciousness of the German public,"[7] despite its continual proclamation in his speeches from 1926 to 1930.[8]

The experiences of the First World War had proved the impossibility of a German victory over a coalition of other great powers that, according to elementary rules of power politics, was almost certain to be formed in response to a German "break-out" to the east or west. Thus, only in an uncommonly narrow ideological perspective was it imaginable to achieve the ultimate objective of Hitler's program by taking on isolated enemies one by one and exploiting current and sometimes serious differences among the other European powers. This was unlikely to occur without the planned "duels" in the form of "lightning wars" provoking premature counter-actions on the part of other states and thus engendering an undesired, unwinnable general war.

Hitler's utterly unrealistic image of Russia can only be called mythical. It was devoid of any comprehension of the actual foundations of the Soviet system. He matched it with a one-sided idealized conception of England, in which only certain elements of British reality—the colonial and maritime traditions—were included. That component of British policy most important in respect to his program—Britain's interest in the continental European balance of power—was ignored. Any German foreign policy based upon such misconceptions was likely to fail fast unless uncommonly favorable conditions in international relations provided a lengthy period for illusory successes. This was precisely the case in the 1930s as, in contrast to the period before 1914, deep antagonisms between Britain and Russia granted Germany a relatively large space for maneuver.

6

HITLER'S FOREIGN POLICY
AND THE ALIGNMENT
OF THE POWERS,
1933–1939

I N a revealing speech to a small circle shortly before the German defeat of France in the spring of 1940, Goebbels triumphantly posed the question that we, looking back at the undisturbed spread of German power from January 1933 to September 1939, constantly ask today: How was it possible that the European states let Hitler have his way for so long until they —and even then only a few of them at first—finally stood up to him in September 1939 when he attacked Poland? It is argued that the far-reaching and radical aims of Hitler's foreign policy were there for the reading—if only *Mein Kampf* had been taken seriously. Reich Propaganda Minister Josef Goebbels could correctly observe on April 5, 1940:

> Up to now we have succeeded in leaving the enemy in the dark concerning Germany's real goals, just as before 1932 our domestic foes never saw where we were going or that our oath of legality was just a trick. We wanted to come to power legally, but we did not want to use power legally . . . They could have suppressed us. They could have arrested a couple of us in 1925 and that would have been that, the end. No, they let us through the danger zone. That's exactly how it was in foreign policy too . . . In 1933 a French premier ought to have said (and if I had been the French premier I would have said it): "The new Reich Chancellor is the man who wrote *Mein Kampf,* which says this and that. This man cannot be tolerated in our vicinity. Either

he disappears or we march!" But they didn't do it. They left us alone and let us slip through the risky zone, and we were able to sail around all dangerous reefs. And when we were done, and well armed, better than they, then they started the war.[1]

As early as February 3, 1933, a few days after assuming office, Hitler had revealed to the army chiefs the outlines of his program. All forces were to be rallied under his leadership with the "sole overall aim of recovering political power" domestically and then turning outward, "perhaps—and no doubt preferably—to conquer new living space in the East and Germanize it ruthlessly." At the same time Hitler had admitted: "The most dangerous period is that of rearmament. Then we shall see whether France has statesmen. If she does, she will not grant us time but will jump on us (presumably with eastern satellites)," that is, together with Poland and Czechoslovakia.[2]

Hitler's concern, still reflected in Goebbels' 1940 speech, came from the knowledge of his own extensive aims. But these were unrelated to the real foreign policy intentions and possibilities of the other powers, whose European and global alignments were determined above all by the tension between the Soviet Union and the "capitalist" nations at the end of the Great Depression. None of the statesmen of this period reckoned seriously with such Hitlerian intentions. The world economic crisis had led the established great powers to a partial retreat from "grand policy" and international obligations. In these years, the League of Nations was already losing its political influence. All states were preeminently concerned with pressing domestic problems. In particular, the great liberal democratic states, England and France, were in this period incapable of political power demonstrations, let alone military action. Since the mid-1920s, France had concentrated on an increasingly narrowly defined policy of security and had withdrawn behind the fortified Maginot Line. England held to her traditional concern for the balance of power with which, however, the realities of Europe since the First World War were not in full accord. To a limited degree, England took up Germany's revisionist demands against a France that appeared overly strong. On the whole, the diplomatic sights of the "capitalist" powers were fixed on the

"inner circle" of London-Paris-Rome-Berlin. Moscow, the pa-
riah, lay outside this circle.

The global political situation was meanwhile marked by the
rupture of America's previously strong financial and economic
ties to Europe, which had greatly contributed to the stabilization of the situation on the continent in the latter half of the
1920s. Isolationism toward Europe, which only now began to
carry the day in America (especially in regard to future military
commitment), was not, however, matched by a comparable
pull-back in the Pacific or East Asia. There, Japan had been the
first great power to break out of the order established in 1919–
1920. In September 1931 Japan launched a policy of expansion
in North China (Manchuria), then in March 1933 withdrew
from the League of Nations. In addition to the United States,
Russia too was particularly attentive to developments in East
Asia in this period. Stalin's fear of a conflict with Japan went a
long way toward determining his European policy at the start of
the 1930s, prompting the conclusion of nonagression pacts with
neighboring Eastern European states. But from the very first, the
basic tendency of Stalin's European policy was to encourage as
far as possible "tensions between the imperialist powers" to
loosen the supposed encirclement of the sole socialist state by
the capitalist powers. Because of the danger of a Far Eastern
war, the central Soviet goal in Europe—the hindrance of any attempted Anglo-French *rapprochement* with Germany—had to
be pursued with special vigor. From this vantage point it was
logical in terms of Soviet German policy for the German Communist Party (KPD), which was fully subservient to Moscow, to
direct its tactics against the parties of the middle and particularly the Socialists (SPD) who were the standard-bearers of the
policy of German accommodation with the West. Conversely,
an assumption of power by Hitler could be expected to negate
the successes of Stresemann's and Brüning's policies toward the
West. So in Stalin's view, Hitler's accession on January 30,
1933, signified not a setback, but a point of departure for tensions that could soon be expected between Hitler and the Western powers.

In the main, these hopes were quickly shattered, necessitating
a change in Soviet tactics. Polish strongman Pilsudski sounded

out Paris about a joint application of pressure against Hitler while the Nazi regime was still insecure. These so-called "preventive war" designs came to nothing because of France's immobility in foreign affairs. Thereupon Pilsudski himself undertook a *rapprochement* with Hitler in May 1933 that in turn must have particularly alarmed the Soviets. The great shift in the methods, though not the aims, of Soviet foreign policy that Stalin then carried out was directed at the Western powers. This shift was characterized by slogans of anti-fascism and "collective security", by Soviet entrance into the League of Nations, and by the pursuit of "United Front" and "Popular Front" tactics. All this was grounded in Stalin's fear that a German-Polish settlement would be followed by an understanding between Hitler and the West on the basis of a common anti-Soviet policy.

While the other powers were uncertain in their attitudes toward the Third Reich, and despite several risks (the sudden withdrawal from the League on October 14, 1933, and the subversive activity of Austrian Nazis), Hitler was able, through unscrupulous and shifting tactics, to overcome the diplomatic isolation that threatened three times: in the autumn of 1933; in the summer of 1934, after the abortive Nazi coup in Vienna; and in the spring of 1935, following the declaration of German military sovereignty. With the conclusion of the Anglo-German Naval Agreement of July 18, 1935, he finally won greater freedom of action in foreign policy. His room for maneuver abroad was considerably broadened thereafter by Italy's Abyssinian war of October 1935 to the summer of 1936 and by the outbreak of the Spanish Civil War in July 1936. The sanctions imposed against Italy by the League of Nations pushed Mussolini into Hitler's arms, while the course of the Spanish Civil War showed that England still perceived her conflict with the Soviet Union, which intervened in Spain, to be of greater consequence than her tensions with the German and Italian "Axis powers" also militarily engaged in Spain. France, however, no longer possessed the strength to realize her own divergent objectives. With the acceptance of Hitler's occupation of the demilitarized zone of the Rhineland on March 7, 1936, France was essentially reduced to following England's lead in foreign policy.

Until Neville Chamberlain's appointment as prime minister in

May 1937, British European policy had been pragmatically decided on a case-by-case basis. Chamberlain's conservative government lent it a certain coherence while, however, misjudging both the dynamism and consistency of Hitler's policies. The foreign policy summed up in the all too simplistic and derogatory term "Appeasement," was based on the deep social and political cleavage between the Soviet Union and the rest of Europe, particularly the powers England, France, Italy, and Germany. Contrary to the claims of Soviet historiography, the point of Appeasement was not to divert Hitler's expansion to the East in order to avoid an impending confrontation between Hitler and the Western powers. It was rather to integrate Germany and Italy in a four-power European order and bind them to a new European system that would replace the Versailles settlement, following the satisfaction of those German revisionist aims that seemed justified (for example, German claims on Austria, the German-speaking Sudetenland, the former German city of Danzig, and increased economic influence in southeastern Europe). To the British government, such a new European order seemed the best security against a direct or indirect Soviet threat. Chamberlain's four-power plan was thus conceived in terms of defense against the East. By tying Germany economically to the West, Britain sought to curb the danger of a violent German expansion to the east and the continental hegemony that would result.

The crucial element in the British strategy was unconditional support of Poland's position as an independent, quasi-great power, for Poland was the most important obstacle to German expansion to the East. Quite apart from the fact that Moscow's partnership was not sought, Soviet strength was held in lowest esteem. By early 1936, even before the Stalinist purges of the Red Army officer corps in 1937–1938, the British government was convinced that Hitler would have little difficulty in rapidly conquering European Russia so long as the Western powers or Poland did not oppose him. The British historian and cultural philosopher Arnold J. Toynbee met with Hitler in February 1936 and sought to probe Germany's Eastern ambitions. He told Hitler: "In a duel between Germany and Russia . . . we expect that Germany would be the winner. Indeed, we expect her victory to be so decisive that it would enable her to annex the Ukraine and the Urals, with their vast agricultural and mineral resources. In that event, Germany would shoot up to the stature of a super-power on the scale of the United States; and then we, Germany's western neighbors, would be overshadowed and dwarfed by this vastly expanded Third German Reich. We might then find ourselves at its mercy."[3] The extraordinarily low estimate of Russian strength on which this prediction was based was maintained by both Hitler and the British government until well into the Second World War.

The year 1936 saw the transition from domestic German reconstruction to the actualization of Hitler's foreign program. Noteworthy in this process was how the floodlights of propaganda were directed at certain distant goals, while the immediate objectives remained in the dark. Before Hitler actually entered upon the first phase of his policy of open expansion in continental Europe, German propaganda already forecast the phase of winning world power. On March 7, 1936, Hitler, for the first time as Reich Chancellor, officially demanded the return of Germany's former African colonies. From then on, this was a recurrent theme in his speeches. Yet he drew back when the British government sought to start concrete colonial negotiations in 1937–1938; the hour for the African land-grab was supposed to strike only after continental hegemony had been won. On March 16, 1939, a day after the occupation of Prague and the creation of the Protectorate of Bohemia and Moravia, Goebbels' instructions to the press hinted vaguely at the long-range aim: "Use of the term 'Greater German World Empire' is undesirable. The term 'World Empire' is reserved for later eventualities."[4] Such a dominion, Himmler told S.S. group leaders on November 8, 1938, would be "the greatest empire that man ever established and the world ever saw."[5]

The most important measure anticipating this last stage of Hitlerian foreign policy, taken on January 27, 1939, was the decision to build a powerful German high seas fleet. By 1944–1946, 10 capital ships, 3 battle cruisers, 8 heavy cruisers, 44 light cruisers, 4 aircraft carriers, 68 destroyers, 90 torpedo boats, and 249 submarines were to be built. With this decision, Hitler broke the 1935 Anglo-German Naval Agreement even before denouncing it officially on April 28, 1939, following England's March 31 guarantee of Polish independence. The decision to build a fleet over a long period had a political implication that Hitler acknowledged to the naval commander-in-chief, Admiral Erich Raeder: until the fleet was completed around 1945, risk of war with Britain had to be avoided at all costs.

The naval construction fit in with the planned sequence of Hitler's program as it had meanwhile been roughly fixed. In his secret memorandum of August 1936 on the Four Year Plan, Hitler reckoned that peaceful means for German expansion would be exhausted by 1940 at the latest. He therefore demanded that in four years' time "the German army be ready for action" and "the German economy capable of waging war."[6] But these pronouncements should not be understood as Hitler's intention to unleash a general war in Europe in 1940. (The main stage of the continental European phase of his program, the conquest of European Russia, was planned for 1943–1945.) Rather, the military and economic measures taken in 1936 were designed to enable Hitler to exert "political pressure up to the threat of war"[7] and pursue an "audacious policy of risk"[8] in accomplishing the intermediate aims of the years 1938–1939. Consequently, a significant, if steadily diminishing, discrepancy always existed between German readiness for war as described in propaganda and the real level of armament achieved. On the basis of the general economic mobilization begun with the Four Year Plan of 1936, which represented a stage between a peacetime and a "total war" economy, Hitler meant to wage distinct, separately timed "lightning wars" against one enemy at a time without bringing on a world war.

In the economic realm, Hitler had already made a basic decision in line with his program when, in the first years of his regime, he declined to lead Germany back into the world economy, then recovering from the great crisis of 1929–1933. To his mind, the inevitably close economic ties with other powers would have meant political dependency and immobility threatening to his program's designs. The economic goal of autarky for Hitler's Reich was to be reached not on the basis of a "Greater Germany" or "Middle Europe," but through the domination of all continental Europe and a "supplementary" African sphere.

The subsequent economic analysis of the Reich's situation at the beginning of the war is not surprising in view of Germany's potential and Hitler's conceptions:

> German industry entered the struggle in 1939 with expanded and modernized capacity and with considerable reserves in the crucial raw materials industries. The clustering of sites in militarily endangered border regions was at least reduced at important junctures. The chance for industrial supremacy was thus present —unless stronger foes entered the war, or the conflict dragged on too long and became a war of mass production. Germany had not rearmed to the extent that others believed, but measured against the armaments of its initial enemies, Germany's were strong and modern enough for a short war. Despite assertions to the contrary in political speeches, preparations for a long war were not taken. German superiority stood and fell with the brevity of the war.[9]

When the war began in September 1939, supplies of raw materials that had to be imported were sufficient for a war of nine to twelve months at most. The expansion of the army and air force was projected over a period lasting until 1942, that is, until just before the date for the drive to the East and the conquest of European Russia.

The phase of open expansion began in 1938–1939. Austria was incorporated into the Reich on March 13, 1938, followed by the Sudetenland after the Munich pact of September 29; the remainder of Czechoslovakia was dismantled on March 15, 1939. From the beginning of this phase, Hitler's basic problem was whether England would accept his step-by-step conquest of the entire continent or, from a certain point on, would intervene to oppose the unfolding of his program. Beginning in late 1937, warnings and misgivings about England's position came from a variety of sources. Some issued from those conservative forces of the German upper stratum (chiefly leading military figures) who, despite criticism of certain aspects of Nazi policy, had promoted Germany's resurgence under Hitler. These leaders supported a foreign policy of moderate territorial revisions in Europe that seemed to coincide with Hitler's aims, at least as represented in his public speeches after 1933. Their opposition was awakened when Hitler (with only a hint at the ultimate goals) revealed his program of expansion to the commanders of the armed forces and Foreign Minister Konstantin von Neurath on November 5, 1937.

Alarms and doubts were also sounded by those German diplomats abroad who had retained a clear sense of reality and, unlike some of their colleagues, did not tell Berlin only what it wished to hear. The German ambassador to Washington, Hans-Heinrich Dieckhoff, belonged to this group urging caution. President Roosevelt's famous Quarantine Speech at Chicago on October 5, 1937, had, for the first time, clearly indicated that political consequences could follow from his outspoken moral disdain for totalitarian and authoritarian regimes in Europe and East Asia. Although nominally the speech was directed more against Japan, whose invasion of China had been launched in July, Dieckhoff, in his incisive report of December 7 on "American Foreign Policy—Isolation or Activity," clearly referred to the dangers accompanying a major shift in the European balance:

> According to all indications, the United States will continue to follow an essentially passive foreign policy as long as Britain is not prepared to become active herself, or as long as the United States is not subjected to intolerable provocation or values which vitally concern the United States are not at stake. Should any of these occur the United States, despite all resistance within the country, will abandon its present passivity. In a contest in which the existence of Great Britain is at stake, America will put her weight into the scales on the side of the British.[10]

The pressing question for Hitler was whether or not England would view its own existence as endangered by the steady growth of the German area of rule in Europe; he had always argued that it would not. This question was approached differently by his chief foreign policy adviser, Joachim von Ribbentrop, whom he had sent as ambassador to London in 1936 to prepare the way for the "grand solution" of global compromise with England. In his "Memorandum for the Führer" on January

2, 1938, Ribbentrop concluded, against Hitler's wishful thinking, that "a change in the status quo in the East to Germany's
advantage can only be accomplished by force" and that in such
a case England would probably intervene. Hence the task at
hand was to erect a worldwide coalition against England. This
meant converting the existing Berlin-Rome-Tokyo political
triangle, heretofore more propagandistic than real, into a military alliance aimed primarily at Britain and, "furthermore, winning over all states whose interests conform directly or indirectly
with ours." Out of regard for Hitler's designs on Russia, Ribbentrop did not refer to the Soviet Union in his memorandum,
but he was clearly thinking in terms of Soviet participation in
the anti-British bloc. By the time of his recall from London Ribbentrop had, in contrast to Hitler, come to see the conflict with
England as the primary one if England could not be reduced by
political means: "Henceforth—regardless of what tactical inter-
ludes of conciliation may be attempted with regard to us—every
day that our political calculations are not actuated by the fundamental idea that England is our most dangerous enemy would
be a gain for our enemies."[11]

Under the influence of Ribbentrop, whom he made foreign
minister on February 4, 1938, Hitler's political attitude toward
Britain grew ambivalent. Although he never truly embraced Ribbentrop's foreign policy—it was, after all, the very opposite of
his own—after mid-1938 Hitler no longer excluded the possibility of a conflict with England in an early phase of his program. Still, he continued to aspire to his "grand solution" of
global Anglo-German compromise and to consider English neutrality attainable during the phase of German continental expansion. On Hitler's orders, the navy and air force began to plan
in mid-1938 for a potential war with England, a contingency
previously ignored. As, however, German rearmament had been
geared solely to continental Europe, the military could only conclude that the technical prerequisites for victory over England
would be lacking for several years.

At the end of March 1939, following the establishment of the
Protectorate of Bohemia and Moravia and the inclusion of Slo-
vakia as a satellite in the German sphere, Hitler realized that he
had exhausted his potential for peaceful expansion, particularly

since his attempt to include Poland as a junior partner in the
German-led continental bloc for the later drive to the East had
now completely failed. Britain's guarantee of Polish independence on March 31, 1939, made this perfectly clear. With often
divergent aims in mind, Hitler and Ribbentrop then turned all
their efforts to the political isolation of Poland, now designated
an enemy, and to her defeat in the localized war that was being
prepared for September 1939.

The European situation had fundamentally changed. Yet despite tactical turnabouts—evident particularly in the Moscow
negotiations begun in April 1939 between the Western powers
and the Soviet Union for a defensive alliance against Hitler—the
two decisive European powers, Britain and Russia, held firmly
to the basic lines of their existing foreign policies. The British
guarantee of the independence, though not the boundaries, of
Poland reflected standing policy, as did the readiness of Chamberlain's government to continue its long pursuit of a European
constellation that would isolate the Soviet Union. Germany and
Italy were to be won over to such an order by further and (by
Britain's if not Hitler's standards) generous concessions. This
emerged clearly during the exceptionally important discussions
between Helmuth Wohlthat, Director of Reich Minister Her-
mann Göring's Four Year Plan staff, and high British officials in
London in July 1939. Britain's newly strengthened desire for
wide-ranging Anglo-German economic cooperation in Europe
and overseas—as part of an overall solution that would include
Danzig's return to the Reich and a revision of the German-Polish border—was also thought of as a means of restraining Hitler
and, in the long run, of making German military expansion impossible. This, of course, was in direct opposition to Hitler's
program.

Stalin, for his part, must have grasped at an early date that,
despite the Moscow negotiations, Chamberlain was still wooing
Hitler's Germany and not the Soviet Union. He discerned that
the negotiations initiated by London and Paris had the sole purpose of pressuring Hitler into a compromise with England on
British terms. Stalin, however, had his own grand design, and
his sole interest lay in reversing this goal of Anglo-German compromise, that is, in sharpening Anglo-German tensions and en-

couraging an open conflict between Germany and the Western powers. This was especially true in the summer of 1939, as war-like incidents flared between Soviet and Japanese troops in the Far East. Stalin must have seen a strong possibility of facing a two-front war against Japan and a Germany diverted—as he always suspected—against the Soviet Union by Great Britain.

The Soviet Union's entrance into the League of Nations in 1934 and the slogan of "collective security" had, in keeping with Stalin's own foreign program, worked against the understanding he feared between Nazi Germany and the West. After the Munich conference, however, Stalin had to consider this approach a failure. With the dismissal on May 3, 1939, of Foreign Minister Maxim Litvinov, the exponent of the previous, seemingly pro-Western side of his policy, Stalin made the change of course he thought necessary. Even in the Litvinov era, he had kept open the possibility of a tactical cooperation with Hitler's Germany aimed against the West. This prospect, as in the years before 1934, again acquired central importance within the context of Stalin's overall—and unchanging—strategy.

Ribbentrop's attempt to transform the Berlin-Rome-Tokyo triangle, loosely held together by the Anti-Comintern Pact of 1936, into a military alliance had meanwhile failed during the summer of 1939. To be sure, the German-Italian "Pact of Steel" signed on May 22 had expressly called for an offensive military alliance between the two Axis powers; but Mussolini limited the alliance to the period after 1942, since Italy's losses in Ethiopia and Spain made any new large-scale Italian military effort impossible for the time being. The anti-British military alliance between Germany and Japan for which Ribbentrop had worked since mid-1938 had also, by August 1939, lost all prospect of success: the Japanese government viewed the Soviet Union as the archenemy and was prepared to enter into an alliance with Germany only if it were directed against Russia. And so the concept of the anti-English Berlin-Rome-Tokyo global triangle, which to Ribbentrop's mind even the Soviets might later join, and which had aimed either to paralyze England in Europe by tying her down in East Asia and the Mediterranean or else to involve her in a three-front war, remained a pipe-dream.

In the summer of 1939, both Hitler's strategy and Ribbentrop's policy toward England were faced with an acute crisis. From this emerged in late July or early August Hitler's decision to make a tactical shift of 180 degrees and strike a deal with Stalin. They would divide the East European *cordon sanitaire*, erected in 1919–1920, into German and Soviet spheres of influence. Hitler expected the British government to be so shaken by the surprise coup that it would suffer Germany's defeat of Poland in an isolated campaign and resign itself to the loss of the Polish "barrier." In other words, Hitler decided to reject the offer Chamberlain deemed generous (the basis of the Wohlthat negotiations), to pursue his own purposes with modified tactics, and to proceed with the inclusion of most of Poland into the German sphere by late summer—either through the submission of the Polish government to his conditions or by force.

7

HITLER, STALIN, AND
THE BRITISH GOVERNMENT:
AUGUST 1939

E VEN as the tactical shift toward an arrangement with the Soviet Union was in full swing, Hitler gave expression to the
constancy of his aims in a conversation of August 11, 1939,
with Carl J. Burckhardt, the High Commissioner of the League
of Nations in the free city of Danzig: "Everything that I under-
take is directed against Russia; if the West is too stupid and too
blind to understand this, then I will be forced to reach an understanding with the Russians, smash the West, and then turn all
my concentrated strength against the Soviet Union. I need the
Ukraine, so that no one can starve us out again as in the last
war."[1] Poland, which Hitler had resolved since the spring to re-
move as an independent power, was no longer even an issue. By
"smashing the West," Hitler meant the defeat of France and the
elimination of all British influence on the continent; both aims
were to be accomplished during the period of détente with Stalin, before the German march to the East. Hitler's argument that
Germany had to rule a blockade-proof area hinted at the more
distant future: the expected confrontation with the sea powers
following the winning of the Ukraine.

The continuity of Hitler's far-reaching strategy is also visible
in his hint of a "generous offer" to England of August 25, 1939,
an offer to come in the period after Poland's fall. Apart from the
tactical motive of having England stand aside during the Polish
campaign, the initiative showed Hitler's continued desire for a

"grand solution" whereby England would let Germany control the continent in return for a German guarantee of the British Empire. His rejection of the British proposals for compromise transmitted through Wohlthat and Göring must be seen in the light of this announcement of his own "generosity" toward England.

On August 25, two days after the conclusion of the German-Soviet Nonaggression Pact, which Hitler expected to have a powerful effect on England, he told the British ambassador, Sir Neville Henderson, that after the Polish question had been resolved, he would "approach England once more with a large and comprehensive offer." He was "ready to conclude agreements with England which . . . would not only guarantee the existence of the British Empire in all circumstances as far as Germany is concerned, but would also if necessary assure the British Empire of German assistance regardless of where such assistance should be necessary."[2]

Like Hitler, the British government and Stalin held true to their respective foreign policy concepts, despite the increasing gravity of the situation after mid-August 1939. Even while concluding a treaty of alliance with Poland on August 25, Britain was ready, as before, to agree to moderate revisions of the German-Polish frontier, particularly in regard to Danzig. Right up to the final days of August, London pursued attempts to set up direct contact between Berlin and Warsaw in the hope of achieving such a settlement. This revision was not designed to pacify Hitler momentarily; it was part of that comprehensive strategy of placing and binding Germany in a European state system to which Chamberlain's government, albeit with increasing doubts of its realization, held fast. The only alternative they saw was the catastrophe of war.

Since early 1939, when serious doubts had been raised as to whether Munich had in fact been, as Chamberlain's government had assumed, a first step toward the success of its strategy, the British government had begun to plan for a possible war with Germany. A basic military plan was drawn up. Planning followed a line of inquiry that reflected the defensive origin of British calculations: Which British positions had to be held at all costs? Here the security of the Atlantic sea lanes connecting the

British motherland with the Commonwealth, the colonies, and America was seen as vital to the maintenance of British power; this was the first task listed in the Admiralty's war plan (approved by the cabinet on January 30) and was characterized as "of the highest importance."[3] Next on this list of wartime priorities came Britain's imperial position in the Mediterranean. There a temporary loss of dominance was viewed as a possibility, but any threat to the Atlantic lanes was to be turned back at all costs by Britain's entire naval and air forces.

In contrast to these well-defined objectives, all other British military planning remained quite variable and, in part, vague. This was true even of the basic plan for military operations on the continent that had been worked out in Anglo-French staff conferences since the spring of 1939. In case of a European war —a growing probability after Germany's occupation of rump-Czechoslovakia on March 15 and Britain's guarantee of Polish independence on March 31—an Anglo-French agreement on the framework for cooperation was hammered out on April 4.[4] Assuming that Germany and Italy would simultaneously open hostilities, and assuming further that they were superior in land and air forces and inferior in sea power and economic potential, the common war plan foresaw a general strategic defensive in the first phase of the war. It was expected that a long war would gradually see the balance shift to the Western powers as a result of their greater productive capacity, backed up by a firm base of supply overseas, especially in America. Despite their opportunities for attack, the Central European enemies appeared boxed-in, as if in a fortress. The Western powers would seize the chance for an early offensive only against the enemy's presumed weakest point, in North Africa. A general offensive against Italy, the weaker partner, would later ensue, followed by a vaguely outlined final attack against Germany itself.

The allies' ultimate political goal was to restore the European balance that Hitler's expansionism had destroyed. Although this seemed to require the elimination of the Nazi regime, the Anglo-French discussions of 1939 left open the question of how that aim was to be realized in practice. A further question was whether it would prove possible to restore the European status quo of 1939, 1938, or 1933 after Hitler's power had reached such heights by 1939. In good part because of Western underestimation of Soviet strength and the failure to perceive the rigid continuity of Stalin's basic policy, this question was never posed with the necessary rigor and its full consequences—especially for Central and Eastern Europe—were never thought through.

On May 4, 1939, the inclusion of Poland in the Anglo-French war plans was discussed for the first time. The British general staff believed that any worthwhile military aid to Poland was either impossible (if only for geographic reasons) or would come too late. It was felt that since Poland's fate would therefore be decided by the outcome of the general war, the war should be waged sensibly in view of Western resources—that is, along the lines of the strategy set down on April 4, by initially taking a defensive posture without regard for the outcome of the German-Polish conflict. For its part, however, the French general staff concluded a military agreement with its Polish counterpart on May 19 that called for a French offensive with approximately forty divisions against the German western border on the fifteenth day of a European war.

When this treaty was concluded, the French government, like the British, still thought it possible to draw the Soviet Union into a coalition against Germany and Italy. But the allied general staffs imputed no great importance to Soviet participation in the imminent land war, given the generally low estimate of the Red Army since the great purges of the officer corps in 1937–1938. So the idea of an alliance with the Soviet Union did not at first enter into allied strategic planning. As a result, the possibility, which emerged in July and became a certainty in August, that Italy, wildly overrated as a military power, would remain neutral in a European war set off by the German-Polish conflict, played a greater role in shaping Anglo-French conduct than did the definitive loss of the Soviet Union as a potential ally. The Hitler-Stalin pact, which Hitler saw as a political bombshell with enormous impact on the Western powers, in fact so little influenced Britain that it occasioned neither a political change of course nor any discernible reorientation of allied strategy in the opening days of the war.

Stalin's decision to take advantage of Hitler's tactical shift and conclude a pact dividing Eastern Europe between them had been in preparation since Munich. A separate treaty with Hitler appeared to Stalin the most suitable means of avoiding an Anglo-German arrangement that in Soviet eyes could only be directed against the Soviet Union. Hitler could only see the pact as encouraging a military action against Poland instead of the "small solution" of English-mediated revisions of the German-Polish border. Stalin must have feared just such a compromise if a British-French-Soviet military alliance had been signed in August 1939, whereas the German attack against Poland was almost certain to set off a war between Hitler and the Western powers. As he declared to Ribbentrop in remarkable openness on the night of August 23–24, Stalin was convinced that "England, despite her weakness, would wage war craftily and stubbornly."[5] With the coming of war between Germany and the West, the prerequisite for the success of Stalin's own foreign policy was fulfilled.

Like Hitler's, Stalin's program had been set down in the 1920s. According to Soviet Communist beliefs, tensions between the imperialist powers would sooner or later be released in war. Instead of this war taking the form of a common front of the capitalist powers against the Soviet Union, the capitalists had to be brought into conflict with each other. Stalin expounded his thesis at a plenary session of the Central Committee of the Soviet Communist Party on January 19, 1925: "Should . . . [such a] war begin, we will not be able to idly stand by. We will have to take part, but we will be the last to take part so that we may throw the decisive weight onto the scales, a weight that should prove the determining factor."[6]

The pact with Hitler on August 23 and the general European war begun by the German attack on Poland (September 1–3) brought two enormously important benefits to the Soviet Union. Enhanced strategic security, now possible through the acquisition of a broad buffer-zone in Eastern Europe, gave the Soviet Union greater political freedom of action worldwide. At the same time, the Soviets were relieved of the fear of a two-front war in Europe and East Asia. The Hitler-Stalin pact forced Japan to accept defeat in the "most difficult and dangerous military conflict between Russia and Japan since 1904,"[7] the battles of the so-called Nomonhan incident on the Manchurian-Mongolian border that had raged since May 11. Now that the Soviet Union was in a position to bring its full power to bear on East Asia, Japan had to accept a *modus vivendi* with Moscow.

Stalin's decision of August 1939 thus put the Soviet Union in the most favorable position it had enjoyed since its creation in 1917. In place of the conception of "capitalist encirclement" that had dominated its policy, there emerged an appreciation of its position as a great power, respected and indeed wooed by all of the participants in the war, its political weight waxing as the war continued and absorbed the energies of the combatant nations.

By way of contrast, Hitler's two decisive maneuvers of August—the conclusion of the pact with Stalin and the announcement of his forthcoming "generous offer" to Britain—proved to be grandiose blunders. On these two elements rested the illusory expectation to which he had clung right up to the British and French declarations of war on September 3: that England would at bottom shrink from intervention in the Polish conflict and come to accept the *faits accomplis* in Eastern Europe. The decision of the British government, encouraged by President Roosevelt, to oppose this first of Hitler's planned localized campaigns (which were timed to precede the march to the East) and thus his entire program, struck at a central axiom of Hitler's foreign policy and the war preparations that had been based on it. As of September 3, Hitler found himself in a general war, which he had intended neither for that time nor in that set of alignments. To that extent—but only to that extent—the notion of a war "forced" upon him* has a certain kernel of truth.

Beginning on September 3, Hitler found himself in a situation where the fronts had, so to speak, been reversed. Great Britain, whose sufferance of his action against Poland Hitler had expected to the last, declared war on Germany and carried France along. Even Italy did not assume the attitude that Hitler, on the basis of his image of Italian fascism and of Axis teamwork (the result of parallel policies after 1936), believed was his due. In fact, there had always been signs of an Italian policy of *sacro*

---

* A preposterous thesis in the American historian David L. Hoggan's sense of the war guilt of British Foreign Minister Lord Edward Halifax.

egoismo toward Nazi Germany, and one cannot speak of political collaboration here in the usual sense of the words. Italy remained a nonbelligerent, and German-Italian relations now reached their nadir, in part because of the Hitler-Stalin pact, which Mussolini condemned on principle. Anti-Comintern partner Japan, which had been totally surprised by the conclusion of the German-Soviet Nonaggression Treaty, declared its strict neutrality in the European war.

Most important, the pact with Stalin, which had not had the original political impact sought by Hitler, gained a central and, for Hitler, wholly unwanted importance with the onset of war: he was now dependent on the very power whose extermination was his great ambition. Without the strategic security in the East and the economic support that the Soviet Union provided Germany, Hitler could not have mastered the situation of the autumn of 1939. Had Moscow joined the British economic blockade against the Reich, the German war economy would have been paralyzed in short order. At the beginning of the war, Germany depended on foreign sources for 80 percent of its rubber, 65 percent of its tin, 70 percent of its copper, 50 percent of its lead, and 25 percent of its zinc—to name only the most important raw materials. True, synthetic fuel and rubber were produced in increasing quantities after September 1939, and a significant portion of the remaining raw materials was imported through expanded deliveries from Southeastern Europe and Scandinavia during the first six months of the war. But for this, the benevolent neutrality of the Soviet Union represented the key political precondition.

Above all, though, the Hitler-Stalin pact went a long way toward counterbalancing Germany's unfavorable geographic position. It allowed Hitler to mass his combined land and air forces on his western border after the rapid defeat of Poland. He was relieved of the pressure of a two-front war as long as the Soviet Union maintained its benevolent attitude. This attitude was less a repayment of the plentiful concessions granted by Hitler during the pact negotiations than the reflection of underlying Soviet interests. It served to shore up the ostensibly weaker capitalist power against the Western powers, particularly France, whose military power was overrated on all sides.

Forced after September 3, 1939, to deal with the Western coalition, Hitler found himself hard pressed at an early stage of his
program, not the least because the build-up of the German
forces, particularly the navy, was by no means completed. He
could escape his predicament only by rapid and risky military
action. Far more than before, he now had to relate each step of
his program to the political and strategic strengths of his present
and potential enemies (above all the United States) if he were
not to fall into ever greater difficulties.

Hitler's broad program of future expansion by stages had excluded any and all contingency planning for a European war
against the Western powers before that war in fact broke out.
Indeed, apart from the plan for the Polish campaign, there existed no general staff guidelines for future operations. Even in
the summer of 1939, Hitler expressly ordered that the German
High Command give no consideration to overall strategy in the
event of war with the West. Rejecting the possibility that the situation of September 3 would result from his attack on Poland,
Hitler had simply not given it the attention it required.

Only in one particular did Hitler gain from the European war
having been ignited by the conflict with Poland. The German-
Polish borders, as drawn by the Versailles Treaty of 1919 and
the division of Upper Silesia in 1921, were felt to be intolerable
by all political forces in Germany and indeed by the German
people as a whole during the period of the Weimar Republic.
There was a general demand for the revision of these frontiers,
especially the return of Danzig and the elimination of the corri-
dor separating East Prussia from the rest of the Reich. Hitler's
1934 pact with Poland was among the least acclaimed of his foreign policy successes in Germany. When he sought the "small
solution" of revised boundaries with Poland, however, he
gained the broadest consensus, and not just within his party.
Even those leading military figures of the old conservative elite
who had planned a coup against Hitler in the autumn of 1938,
when the Sudeten crisis threatened to ignite a European war,
saw his demands against Poland as justified. In addition, conservative diplomats and army leaders mistook the Hitler-Stalin
pact for a renewal of Bismarck's Russian policy; from their historical standpoint, too, the defeat of the Polish state formed at
Germany's and Russia's expense in 1919–1920, and the rees-

tablishment of a German-Russian border in Poland, seemed desirable. Warsaw's strict refusal to negotiate revisions with Hitler was not understood in Germany. "We believe we will make quick work of the Poles, and, in truth, we are delighted at the prospect. That business *must* be cleared up." So wrote General Eduard Wagner, staff chief to the Army Quartermaster-General, to his wife on August 31, 1939.[8] Wagner was anything but an uncritical supporter of Hitler; he was, on the contrary, one of the leaders of the officers' *fronde*.

With his tactic of making seemingly liberal offers to Poland, Hitler sought to arouse the impression that he was striving for "reasonable" border revisions so that the public would blame Polish intransigence for the war. The result was an enormous propaganda success within Germany and, to a certain degree, even abroad in the West—in France, for example, under the slogan, *"Mourir pour Danzig?"* Resonances of such a short-sighted view of the war's origins may be discerned today in the so-called revisionist historiography of David L. Hoggan, A. J. P. Taylor, and their German imitators in radical right circles. On August 29, however, Hitler had already decided the sequence of events of the next few days, in case a Polish negotiator should yet appear in Berlin. Army Chief of Staff General Franz Halder noted tersely and unequivocally in his diary: "August 30, Poles in Berlin. August 31, collapse of negotiations. September 1, use of force."[9]

Yet the campaign against Poland that began on September 1 was a mere preliminary. In no sense was it *the* war that Hitler sought as the crucial stage in the realization of his program. To his mind, the European war that came on September 3 was as incomprehensible as it was contrary to his aims. The interests of France and England, he thought, were unaffected by the "clearing up" of a regional problem. Instead, they intervened to stop him.

Hitler's responsibility for the war would be quite insufficiently revealed by focusing exclusively on his role in unleashing the European war in August and September 1939. His decision for a second war, totally different in character, must be brought into the picture. This war began with the attack on the Soviet Union on June 22, 1941. Only then did the Second World War truly begin.

8

HITLER'S ROAD
TO HIS WAR,
1940–1941

T HE great gamble in the war that Hitler believed had been forced upon him began with the German offensive in the West on May 10, 1940. There Hitler had three closely related aims:

1. To drive France from the field and at the same time come to an understanding with the French regime to neutralize its fleet (which was out of the range of German arms) and, if possible, France's colonial empire as well.

2. To sound out England early along, even during the campaign, about a global "grand solution," a compromise on his terms, while England was under the direct effect of France's defeat.

3. To strengthen those American forces calling for a restriction of U.S. foreign military engagements to the Western hemisphere. The nature of the defeat of France, the ceasefire, the compromise with England, and propaganda aimed at American public opinion (interpreting the Monroe Doctrine as "America for Americans; Europe for Europeans") would all work to this effect.

These three aims were designed to bring about the political and strategic prerequisites for Hitler's drive to the East. To his way of thinking, he stood in June 1940 at a point that, according to his original rough timetable, he had aimed to achieve by 1943. The situation called for pushing on with his program.

As State Secretary for the Foreign Ministry Freiherr Ernst von Weizsäcker summed up Hitler's appraisal of the situation on June 30, 1940, England needed at most one more "demonstration of our military power before she gives up and leaves us free in the rear for the East."[1] On May 21, as German tanks were breaking through to the Channel, Hitler had already declared that "we want to sound out England on dividing the world."[2] And on June 2, in staff quarters of Army Group A in Charleville he voiced his expectation that Britain would surely now be ready for a "reasonable peace agreement" so that his "hands would finally be free" for his "great and real task: the confrontation with Bolshevism."[3]

On July 3, a few days after the conclusion of the Franco-German armistice, the general staff began, for the first time, preliminary consultations concerning a campaign against Russia.[4] These plans reveal the German assessment of Russian strength, which, even after the basic alteration of the overall picture a few weeks later, remained in force until the beginning of hostilities in the East in June 1941.

The chief of the general staff instructed the Operations Department that the basic question of planning was "how to strike a military blow against Russia so as to force its recognition of Germany's dominant role in Europe."[5] The study for an Eastern campaign completed by Maj. General Marcks on August 5, 1940, assumed that nine weeks at best, and seventeen at worst would suffice to defeat the Red Army and occupy the country up to a line extending from the lower Don, through the middle Volga, to the Northern Dvina. It was believed that the areas most important to the war economy would thereby be in German hands, since—according to the study—"the eastern industrial areas are not yet sufficiently productive." Although the Russians were not expected to "do us the favor of launching an attack," it was felt that they would have to stand and fight in defense of their industrial region west of the Dnieper. So a Russian withdrawal into the nation's inner reaches, as in 1812, seemed out of the question. German planners saw no need to take account of the Red Army's reserves, estimated at eight to twelve million, as the Soviet system was believed incapable of rapidly mobilizing and transporting these forces to the front.

"Since the Russians will not have numerical superiority this time as they did in the world war," Marcks concluded, "it is to be expected that once their lines are broken through, they will quickly succumb to the superiority of German troops and leadership."[6] Such blindness to reality—to sum up the German calculations—informed all further campaign planning as well until the attack began on June 22, 1941.

Considering the dubious grounds for judgment (reliable information was available only on those areas annexed by the Soviet Union since 1939), the carelessness and superficiality of military planning for the Eastern campaign is difficult to comprehend. In contrast, the strike against France was meticulously prepared during the winter of 1939–1940. No one opposed Hitler when he boasted on December 5, 1940, that the Russian army could be "cut to pieces" and "throttled in sections."[7] For the second phase of the Eastern campaign, after a line from the Dnieper to Lake Peipsi had been reached, only "tank thrusts" were envisaged to "clear the debris and secure important strongpoints."[8] Like the general staff, Hitler was convinced that the Red Army and the entire Bolshevist apparatus would collapse during the first phase of the campaign.

Doubtless the general feeling of triumph that reigned after the defeat of France, supposedly the premier military power on the continent, contributed to German overconfidence. Since the First World War, all army and general staff designs had been bound by the strategic triangle of France-Czechoslovakia-Poland. When this enclosure was finally destroyed in the summer of 1940, and the way seemed open for vaster operational planning, the strategic calculations of the German general staff took place as if in uncharted spaces, with all its measurements awry. The sudden release from the confines of Central Europe seemed to demolish all previously valid concepts of German power and military possibilities. But this alone cannot account for the fatal underestimation of the Red Army, as there was no comparably consistent misperception of British and American strength.

A variety of factors combined to form this utterly incongruous misjudgment of Soviet potential: cultural arrogance toward the "inferior" Russians; anti-Communist wishful thinking, which led to an underestimation of the stability of the Soviet system and the effectiveness of its army; the generalization of experiences with the Russian enemy during the First World War; conclusions drawn from the purges of the Soviet officer corps; and finally, misconceptions drawn from the course of the Soviet-Finnish winter conflict. Hitler himself gave this scorn its clearest expression when he told an army adjutant: "We will be in Petersburg in three weeks."[9] The Red Army, he remarked to the Bulgarian envoy in Berlin, was "no more than a joke."[10]

Remarkably, Stalin for his part underestimated German potential to a similar degree once the war entered a new phase in late July 1940. For by then it was clear that Great Britain—contrary to Hitler's original expectations and Stalin's fears after the French campaign—would not give up and reckoned instead on increased American backing.

On July 31, 1940, Hitler for the first time clearly revealed to his military advisers his conclusions regarding the new situation: England's hope lay with the United States and Russia.[11] (This was true of the former, though not of the latter except perhaps for a short period in the early summer of 1940.) Hitler correctly doubted that Germany's limited sea and air power could bring England to terms; and since the United States was out of his reach, he could seek to eliminate that major adversary only by indirect means. The one way to do that, he supposed, was by excluding England's second "hope," Russia, which he feared might be brought into the fray by the sea powers as a "continental spearhead" against Germany or Japan. Hitler calculated that the destruction of the Soviet Union would at once deprive Britain of its last prospect for support in Europe and elevate Japan's status as a power in East Asia. Thus America, threatened from the Pacific, would be paralyzed in the Atlantic and forced to come to terms with the new order dominated by Germany and Japan in the Eastern Hemisphere.

As late as the first weeks of July 1940, Hitler had thought of the attack on Russia solely in the context of his original aims: as the conquest to follow a compromise with England, completing his dominance of continental Europe. After late July, however, it became crucially important to him also as a step toward making England ready for peace and turning the entire war to his advantage. This objective, it seemed to him, could now hardly be

achieved in any other way in view of America's approaching
entry into the war. England's stiff resistance with American support had thus led to a reversal of Hitler's earlier strategy. Previously, the defeat of France and the desired compromise with
Britain were to create a solid strategic base from which to march
east when the moment seemed right. Now his ultimate goal, the
conquest of the East, became in addition a means of coping with
the English-speaking powers, which were not only unwilling to
accept his rule of Central and Western Europe, but were fighting
him over it.

To be sure—and this was decisive for both the character and
the outcome of the Eastern war—the campaign against the Soviet Union, now set for May 1941, did not simply become a
means for ending the war in the West. It was still defined in
terms of the aims of Hitler's original program. In his view, the
initial and constant aim of the Eastern war and the means for
dealing with the concrete situation of the Western war of 1940–
1941 now converged.

Neither the one nor the other were perceived by Stalin as
Hitler's real strategy. Once it became clear that England would
persevere and America would enter the war in due course, Hitler
appeared tied down in the West, faced with an escalating war
with the sea powers. So Stalin believed himself to be in an extraordinarily advantageous position. Here the crucial difference
between Stalin and Hitler can be seen. Stalin never made decisions of "grand policy" on the basis of Bolshevist revolutionary
ideology. He practiced above all a rationally calculated power
politics with the aim of expanding the Soviet empire by exploiting the war that began in 1939 among the "imperialist" powers.
Social revolutionary transformation in newly won territories
was subordinated to strategic security. Hitler, on the other
hand, in the decisive phase of the war in 1940–1941, despite an
alignment of powers different from that foreseen in his program,
abandoned Machiavellian methods of "grand policy" in favor
of the immediate realization of his ultimate racial-ideological
aim.

Stalin saw clearly that the longer the war in the West dragged
on, the weaker Hitler's position was bound to be, particularly as
Anglo-American potential was brought to bear. He also cor-

rectly calculated the German war effort's growing dependency on Soviet economic and political assistance and expected to be able to exact a high price from Hitler for continued Soviet goodwill in the second phase of the war.

But in his rational appraisal of the situation, Stalin could not understand that things looked different to Hitler. He did not know how little Hitler esteemed Soviet military strength. And he could hardly imagine that Hitler believed that in defeating the Soviet Union—even before the conclusion of the war in the West—he had found a solution that not only accorded with the aims of his program but also promised to solve all his problems with relative ease. It did not occur to Stalin that this could be an alternative for Hitler to a new German-Soviet political arrangement that would allow further Soviet territorial gains. He thought such a deal necessary to Germany's effective continuation of the Western war. For Hitler, however, the price was too high.

This mutual underestimation on the part of both Hitler and Stalin was not really the result of their misunderstanding each other's aims. Stalin knew that Hitler sought to attack the Soviet Union in the end. Hitler knew that, in the final phases of the "imperialist" war in Europe, Stalin aspired to seize territories deemed essential to a broadly conceived Soviet policy of security. Their mutual disdain was more a consequence of their ideologically grounded misperceptions of the respective strengths of the National Socialist and Bolshevist systems. Stalin miscalculated so far as to reveal his future aims with brutal openness during Foreign Minister V. M. Molotov's visit to Berlin on November 12–13, 1940. The primary Soviet objectives (Finland, Rumania, Bulgaria, the Turkish straits) were, to be sure, based on the defensible negotiating position that Hitler had to pay a price for a continued and successful war against Britain. But the Soviet Union's outspoken interest, looking to the third and final phase of the war, in Hungary, Yugoslavia, western Poland, Sweden, and the Baltic Sea outlets (The Sound, Skagerak, Kattegatt)[12] could no longer be seen as a price that a victorious Germany could pay. These demands bore no relationship to Soviet security vis-à-vis a powerful Germany oriented to the continent; rather, they anticipated a situation in which the Anglo-Saxon sea powers had taken up position in Western Europe or were about to do so. The realization of these aims presupposed Germany's defeat at the hands of the Western powers. From the standpoint of Soviet security, and especially in light of Russian experiences in the Crimean War and the War of Intervention (1918–1919), Soviet control over access to the Black and Baltic Seas and a shift in its strategic perimeter on the continent with Germany's forced displacement to the West were absolute necessities.

In 1940, neither Hitler nor the British regime was in a position to secure Soviet entry into the war on its side, be it through political concession, by negotiations for an alliance, or by pressure. But either was certainly capable of creating a new situation by taking military action against the Soviet Union. Uncertainty about Stalin's conduct led the British, first in the spring of 1940, and as late as May–June 1941, to make preparations for a bombardment of the Baku oil region.[13] For Britain, a military strike against a Soviet Union intensifying its alliance with Hitler (as London feared to the last) remained, until the morning of June 22, 1941, a serious alternative to the sending of limited assistance to a Soviet Union under German attack.

After securing his Eastern European buffer by treaties with Hitler (1939–1940), Stalin intended to remain aloof from the "imperialist" war between Germany and the West. Only later, at the least possible risk, would he seize those territories that he, anticipating the future growth of Anglo-American power in Western Europe, believed essential to Soviet strategic security and extension of Soviet political influence. All this was contravened by the German attack of June 22, 1941. The assault forced the Soviet Union out of its political waiting game and into a struggle for its survival at a time when Stalin estimated the Red Army, despite rapid rearmament, not yet ready for a major war. Thus two expansionistic, ideological programs of war aims faced each other in 1940–1941, at odds not only in their principles, but also in their opposing thrusts in Eastern Europe.

In this confrontation, it was the Nazi program, propelled by Hitler's frenzy and dependent on the element of surprise and lightning speed for the enactment of its various stages, that struck the first blow. The Bolshevist program for conquering

Eastern Europe was, according to Stalin's patient, cautious policy, set for a later time, after Germany's exhaustion in the Western war. Thus this Soviet program was concealed even as in the following period some of its important elements were altered to fit the new situation of quasi-alliance with the Western powers. Taken as a whole, it could then be portrayed by the Soviets as a reaction to the German attack. The central aim, however—the expansion of the Soviet sphere in Europe to front the Anglo-American sea powers after Germany's defeat—was recognizable from the autumn of 1940 and remained constant.

To a decisive extent, the nature of the war unleashed by Hitler on June 22, 1941, enabled Stalin to attain his goal. Even today, just as it was in many accounts at the time, Operation Barbarossa, as it was called, is often misunderstood and misinterpreted in three ways:

1. As an effort of pure power politics, which arose solely from the needs of the European war underway since September 1939.

2. As a crusade against Stalinist Bolshevism, whose barbaric excesses in the 1930s had unleashed worldwide horror and loathing (the Stalinist terror had indeed overshadowed that of the Nazis before 1939).

3. As a national uprising, under German leadership, of the territories from Finland down to the Black Sea pressured since 1939–1940 by the culturally "inferior" yet far more numerous "half-Asiatic" Russians.

This treble misunderstanding brought Hitler support for Operation Barbarossa not only in Germany, but from a wide range of European states, including areas occupied by Germany and even from within the Soviet Union. Hitler's abuse of these circumstances deserves to be considered one of the determining factors in the history of the Eastern war, together with the radical form of the war of annihilation that began with Hitler's unilateral suspension of the basic rules of warfare on the first day of the campaign.

The Western war remained largely within conventional bounds because the laws of war and nations were accepted in principle on both sides, despite innumerable specific infringements. That the Eastern war was different from the outset was

grasped by neither the German people nor even the vast majority of the German soldiers involved. A form of self-inflicted
blindness, though, afflicted leading military figures who could
have known better. The connection between the apparently
conventional battle at the front and the war of annihilation in
the rear war-zone, as later in those territories placed under civilian rule, was clearly recognizable from several basic orders issued by Hitler.

He after all did disclose his purposes in the Eastern war with
rare openness before at least 200 high-ranking officers at a general assembly on March 30, 1941. Those purposes were in full
disregard of military ethics.[14] Certainly many of those present
shared the view—strongly articulated by a certain Lt. Col. Hen-
ning von Tresckow—that if international law were to be broken in the coming campaign, the Russians should be the first to
break it.[15] This directly contradicted Hitler's fanatical intent to
start his coveted war of extermination himself. The war in the
East, he told the officers, would distinguish itself from that in
the West from the first moment: "Bolshevism is antisocial crimi-
nality . . . The Communist has never been a comrade and will
never be a comrade. We have a war of annihilation on our
hands. If we do not conceive of it as such, we shall indeed defeat
the enemy, but in thirty years the Communist foe will face us
again. We are not waging war to preserve the
enemy . . . Commissars and GPU officials are criminals and
must be treated as such."[16] So ran the notes taken by General
Halder on Hitler's speech to his top brass. The Commander-in-
Chief of the Army, General Walther von Brauchitsch, failed to
register with Hitler the protest that several generals urged.

Four motives intermingled in Hitler's conceptions of his Eastern war:

1. To exterminate the "Jewish-Bolshevik" leadership, including its presumed source, the millions of Eastern European Jews;

2. To win colonial territory for German settlers in what were
deemed Russia's best areas, as well as in those regions that
Hitler thought indispensable for political and strategic reasons;

3. To subjugate the Slavic masses under German rule in four
separate "Reich Commissariats" (for the Baltic states, the
Ukraine, "Muscovy," and the Caucasus) with the main task of

eliminating all memory of the Russian state among the masses and dulling them into blind allegiance to the new overlords;

4. To round out an autarkic, blockade-proof continental European sphere, for which the conquered East represented an inexhaustible reservoir of raw materials and foodstuffs necessary and sufficient for the "Germanic Reich of the German Nation" to sustain the war against the Anglo-Saxon powers and stand up to any conceivable new world war ("Europe autarkic, so to hell with America"—as General Eduard Wagner tersely put it in a private letter of September 20, 1941).[17]

All four tasks were initiated on the first day of the campaign. Here the parallel between the launching of the war against the Soviet Union and the beginning of the "final solution of the Jewish question"—the liquidation of the Jews in German-ruled Europe—deserves special attention. Hitler's struggle against both Bolshevism and the Jews had now moved from the stage of agitation in the 1920s through the stage of political struggle (in the broadest sense of the term) after 1933 to, finally, this ultimate step of extermination on June 22, 1941. Just how close Hitler kept to his axioms of the 1920s, which he was now following to their practical conclusion, is seen in his statement to the Croatian puppet, Marshal Kvaternik on July 21, 1941:

> The Jews are the scourge of mankind . . . If the Jews had free reign, as in the Soviet paradise, they would put the most outrageous schemes into practice. That was how Russia became a plague for mankind . . . Even if only one state, for whatever reason, were to tolerate a Jewish family in it, this would become the bacillus for renewed decay. The unity of the European states would no longer be disturbed if there were no more Jews in Europe. It didn't matter where one sent the Jews, to Siberia or Madagascar. He [Hitler] would approach each state with this demand.[18]

Ten days later, Goering empowered Heydrich in Hitler's name "to make, in concert with the appropriate German central authorities, all requisite preparations for a total solution of the Jewish question in the German sphere of influence in Europe."[19]

As the three million soldiers of the German Eastern army crossed Soviet borders to eliminate the Red Army as a military factor, they were followed by the notorious "task forces" (*Einsatzgruppen*) of the Security Police and the Security Service (SD) of the SS, whose fury consumed more than a half million West Russian Jews in the next months. Thus began the first, East European, phase of the "final solution." As noted above, Hitler followed it with the start of the second, Central and West European, phase on July 31, 1941, at a moment of seeming triumph over the Soviet Union. Phase two was to have proceeded in tandem with the expansion of the area under German control and the final securing of the giant German sphere. Even after the failure of Operation Barbarossa, however, phase two continued almost to completion in the isolation of the extermination camps in Poland until autumn 1944.

Hitler's scheme for the Eastern war represented an attempt, largely realized in the occupied areas, to transfer aims and methods heretofore common only in non-European colonial warfare to a conflict between two European great powers. He combined these with methods of exterminating domestic enemies that had been practiced in Soviet Russia after 1917 and Nazi Germany after 1933. For the first time, an enemy great power was not simply to be reduced to a middle-level power incapable of pursuing "grand policy" and, for a certain time, brought into a state of dependency on the victor through annexations of border zones, the sub-division of territories, or strict economic subordination of the residual state to the victor: these were the accepted political objectives of the imperialist era since the beginning of the First World War. Rather, the conquered state was to be reduced to the level of a colony in every respect. This was the ultimate exaggeration of imperialism.

Barbarossa was only one—though by far the most important —part of Hitler's improvised war plan of late autumn 1940, which foresaw what might be called a "global lightning war" in the Eastern Hemisphere for 1941. This was to have proceeded in the following stages:

1. Soviet Russia would be defeated in a campaign of three, or at most, four months, with the actual decision expected in the first month. The majority of infantry divisions of the Eastern army were therefore scheduled to be withdrawn in August 1941, with motorized units and armored divisions following in

September—all to be reassigned to other arenas. Only fifty to sixty divisions would remain in the East to occupy the territory up to a line stretching from Astrakhan to Archangel; these could also be used for raids up to and beyond the Urals.

2. A three-pronged pincers operation in the Mideast would begin in autumn 1941: one thrust through the Caucasus into Iran; one from Bulgaria, through Turkey, and toward Syria and Iraq; and the third from Libya, over Egypt, Suez, and Palestine, and likewise into the British sphere in the Mideast. Further, a base of operations would be established in Afghanistan to threaten India, the "heart of the British Empire."

3. As early as May 1941, if possible, Japan would drive south to overrun Singapore and threaten India from the east. The Philippines would be avoided to keep America from intervening in an Anglo-Japanese war. (Hitler discussed this plan in February and March 1941 with Japanese Ambassador Oshima and then with visiting Foreign Minister Matsuoka, but the Japanese government would not commit itself to either the strategy or the timing.)

4. Also in the fall of 1941, Gibraltar would be seized, with or without Franco's approval. The Mediterranean would thus be closed to the west and a German bastion in Northwest Africa constructed with Vichy French help (in Morocco and possibly Dakar) to confront America.

9

HITLER'S WORLD POLICY
FROM TRIUMPH
TO CATASTROPHE

T HE first weeks of the Russian campaign seemed not only to fulfill but to surpass Hitler's grand expectations. As early as July 3, Chief of the General Staff Halder noted in his diary: "I am not likely saying too much if I maintain that the campaign against Russia was won inside of fourteen days." Operations against the British in the Mideast could therefore "move to the foreground."[1] Thinking himself on the brink of success in the East, Hitler turned his attention in mid-July to the Anglo-Saxon powers and his next great step, the expansion and securing of the German sphere to the southeast (the Mideast and Southwest Asia) and the southwest (Northwest Africa). On July 14 he had the focus of German rearmament switched from the army to the construction of a powerful air force and a strong submarine fleet.[2]

Not only had the Eastern campaign begun well in Hitler's view, but American and Japanese reaction to it seemed to match his intentions and expectations. While Roosevelt's policy of ever-greater support for Britain, in effect since the summer of 1940, had gradually won wide approval in American public opinion and Congress, the German-Soviet war unleashed a new isolationist wave from a variety of sources. Opposition to Roosevelt's strategy of "involvement short of war" intensified.

Japanese intentions, however, ran less clearly to Hitler's advantage. True, the decision of the Japanese leadership on July 2,

1941 (unknown to him) not to proceed militarily against the Soviet Union—at least until it was no longer a serious factor—but
rather to expand southward with the occupation of southern In-
dochina was in accord with Hitler's own aims. This step, when
taken in late July 1941, brought forth the desired heightening of
tensions in the Pacific. But more decisive was the belief (similarly
hidden from Hitler) of the Japanese naval command, now in an
ascendent position within Japanese ruling circles, that England
and America could not be separated politically or militarily and
that therefore a Japanese attack against Singapore alone was out
of the question. It was considered in Japan's interest to seek a
possible *modus vivendi* with the United States in the coming
months, while Japan enjoyed a position of strength by having
been relieved (by the German-Soviet war) of a possible Russian
front. However, should the United States fail to recognize Japanese leadership of the East Asian sphere, Japan would take advantage of the favorable international conjuncture and, without
concern for the interests of its German ally, risk war against
both America and Britain.

Against this background, Ribbentrop's attempt (begun on
June 28, 1941, initially without Hitler's approval) to instigate a
Japanese declaration of war on the Soviet Union could only fail.
Ignorant of the decision already taken by Japan, Ribbentrop in-
tensified his efforts on July 10 by ordering the German ambassa-
dor in Tokyo, Eugen Ott, to

> Go on with your efforts to bring about the earliest possible par-
> ticipation of Japan in the war against Russia . . . The natural
> goal must be, as before, to bring about the meeting of Germany
> and Japan on the Trans-Siberian Railroad before winter sets in.
> With the collapse of Russia, the position of the Tripartite Powers
> in the world will be so gigantic that the question of the collapse
> of England, that is, the absolute annihilation of the British Isles,
> will only be a question of time. An America completely isolated
> from all the rest of the world would then be faced with the sei-
> zure of those of the remaining positions of the British Empire im-
> portant to the Tripartite Powers.[3]

In this moment of seeming triumph in the East, Hitler went,
for a moment, beyond the bounds of the objectives set in his
program. On July 14, 1941, he proposed, in the most concise

form, a comprehensive war alliance between Germany and Japan. He told Japanese Ambassador Oshima: "In its new imperialist spirit, America is pressuring now the European, now the East Asian living space. From our point of view, Russia is the threat in the east, America in the west; from that of Japan, Russia in the west, America in the east. He [Hitler] is therefore of the opinion that we must annihilate them together. In the lives of nations there are hard tasks that one could not solve by shutting oneself off from their existence or by putting them off to a later time."[4]

Meanwhile, as long as the Soviet campaign continued, Hitler wanted at all costs to avoid a conflict with the United States. On July 25, he announced to Raeder that he "was holding armed action against the United States in reserve until the end of the Eastern campaign."[5] The Americans, whose forces had occupied Iceland on July 7, would then have to "get out, even if he had to fight for years."[6] Even before the beginning of the Eastern campaign—first in the autumn of 1940, then on May 22, 1941—Hitler had spoken of an occupation of the Azores as a base from which to "deploy long-distance bombers against the United States beginning in the fall [1941]."[7]

Optimism concerning the Eastern front still reigned on July 23. "In approximately one month," Halder noted for his briefing of that day, "we may assume that our troops will be in the vicinity of Leningrad and Moscow, and along a line from Orel to the Crimea; by early October at the Volga, and in November in the Caucasus from Batumi to Baku."[8] On July 8 Hitler had repeated his previously announced determination to raze Moscow and Leningrad to the ground in order to avoid survivors "whom we would have to feed in winter."[9] He spoke of his intention to bring about a "catastrophe" for the Russian people that would "rob not only Bolshevism but also Muscovy of its core."[10] He would intensify the ongoing war of annihilation— the systematic mass murders by the *Einsatzgruppen* that had raged behind the lines from the onset of the campaign—by extending it to the Slavic masses, reducing them by millions.

But the optimism of July gave way to a quite different appraisal of the Eastern front in August, first by the Army Chief of Staff and then to some degree by Hitler. By the end of July, the other side had clearly recognized Hitler's war of annihilation for what it was: a programmatic effort and not simply the excesses that might accompany a military struggle. This led to a stiffening of the Red Army's resistance and consolidation of Stalin's shaken rule. Hitler's extermination campaign liberated elemental energies in Russia that, seeking to ward off threatened enslavement by the foreign conqueror, rose in defense of the fatherland and so contributed to the stabilization of Stalin's totalitarian Communist regime.

Only because of the genocidal nature of the German assault could Stalin's July 3 call for partisan resistance succeed. To be sure, the partisan activity that grew from month to month reflected both Bolshevik military theory and Russian tradition. But the scale of partisan warfare in the East is explicable only as a reaction to Hitler's war of extermination. Within a few weeks, "German policy was already marked beyond reversal by the large-scale murder of uncounted prisoners of war and the systematic extermination campaign waged by the SD's *Einsatzgruppen*."[11]

By late July, stiffened Soviet resistance had already forced the first postponement in the timetable for the Eastern war. This instantly affected wider strategic planning, as the advances on Libya and the British position in the Mideast had to be scratched for 1941. In August, the slow progress of the campaign necessitated further cancellations. In the High Command's August 27 memorandum, "The Strategic Situation in Late Summer 1941,"[12] it was acknowledged for the first time that no troops from the Eastern front could be spared for other theaters that autumn. Thus the planned conquest of Gibraltar and the seizure of a German bastion in Northwest Africa (including the outlying Portuguese and Spanish islands) were now abandoned.

Hitler's subsequent return to the basic line of his original program is largely to be understood in the context of this greatly (if not yet decisively) altered appraisal of the Eastern front. As he told confidants on September 10 and Italian Foreign Minister Ciano on October 25, the final confrontation between the world powers America and Germany would await the next generation. "I will not live to see it," he told a trusted circle in his headquar-

ters (at that time when a great encircling battle east of Kiev
seemed to him to pave the way for a decisive turn in the campaign), "but I am happy for the German people, who will one
day see England and Germany oppose America together. Germany and England will know what each has to expect from the
other. And then we will finally have found the right ally."[13]
While German armies advanced on Moscow, and while he was
already discussing the use of Italian troops in the Caucasus and
subsequently in a campaign through Iran and Afghanistan to
India, he declared to Count Ciano that "a later generation
would have to deal with the problem of Europe versus America.
It will then not be a matter of Germany or England, or Fascism,
National Socialism, or opposing systems, but of the common interests of all . . . within the European economic region and its
African appendages."[14]

In November 1941, as the Eastern campaign bogged down,
Hitler showed his first traces of resignation. In a statement to his
inner circle on November 19, taken down by Halder, he surprised his listeners with his "expectation . . . that the recognition that the two opposing blocs were incapable of defeating
each other would lead to a negotiated peace."[15] "We must face
the possibility," Halder concluded, "that neither of the two
main enemies [meaning Germany and England] will succeed in
destroying or decisively wearing down the other."[16] Thus had a
point been reached in the German leadership's appraisal of the
Second World War that bears comparison with the judgment by
Falkenhayn and Bethmann Hollweg in November 1914 of Germany's situation in the First World War.[17]

From Hitler's insight, however, reemerged the illusion that by
renouncing intended gains from the West (the British Mideast
and Northwest Africa) he could come to a compromise with
Britain after all. On December 7, 1941, even as Japanese bombers embarked against the American fleet at Pearl Harbor, Hitler
spoke of his hope to "enter into talks with England at France's
expense."[18]

By late November, he already knew that Japanese-American
negotiations had broken down and that an outbreak of war in
the Pacific that would involve America was therefore likely.
Here too Hitler resigned himself to the inevitability of American

entry into the war at a most undesirable time. Still, in the current situation—the failure not just of Barbarossa but of the entire improvised war plan of late 1940—America's being forced to fight in two theaters was the lesser of two evils to Hitler. The alternative of a Japanese-American accord, which had remained possible for many weeks, would have had the consequence of shifting the weight of American power to the Atlantic and Europe.

Nevertheless, Hitler's declaration of war on the United States on December 11, 1941, which followed the Japanese attack on the Pacific territories of Britain and the United States, was not an objective foreign policy move. Nor was it a deliberate, major resolution in any way comparable to the decision for the Eastern war. Rather, it was a gesture designed to conceal the fact that he could no longer control the direction of the war that had laid his plans to waste. His admission to Japanese Ambassador Oshima on January 3, 1942, that he did "not yet" know "how America could be defeated" speaks for itself.[19]

His sole remaining chance to regain the military initiative, at least in the Eastern Hemisphere, was a combined German-Japanese effort in Southwest Asia and India to follow the expulsion of the Red Army from the Don and Volga region and a German advance over the Caucasus. But the opportunity, which seemed real in early 1942, passed; after the costly winter battles on the Eastern front, Hitler was in no position to mount a new offensive on its southern flank until late June. By then, Japanese offensive power had already been largely broken at the sea and air battle of Midway in early June.

The offensive in the West, delineated in the plans and proposals drawn up in the autumn and winter of 1940–1941, was to set the stage for a German position of world power in the Mideast and Northwest Africa. With the failure of Operation Barbarossa, it too became a dead letter. As a result, Germany's struggle against the Anglo-Saxon powers maintained its defensive character for the duration of the war. In failing to achieve a successful and timely end to the Eastern war, Hitler lost the flexibility he had sought for the realization of his broader strategy. After a quick defeat of the Soviet Union, he had planned to face the world from a cohesive world power position in Europe,

North Africa, and the Mideast. Instead, he faced combined
Anglo-American power in the West from a partially secured, improvised "fortress" in Europe's heartland, while the war in the
East, which he himself had unleashed, rebounded upon Germany.

Hitler's last attempt to "twist fate" (to borrow a term from
General Alfred Jodl, Hitler's chief operations adviser) failed
with the summer offensive in the East in 1942. From September
1942 on, Hitler saw himself in the role of the Third Army Command of the First World War. He drew the parallel himself in his
order concerning the "Basic Tasks of Defense" of September
8.[20] Memories of the nature of the material struggle on the
Western front in 1914–1918 determined the obdurate resolve
to hold all positions that characterized both his general strategy
and specific military tactics. As Jodl admitted shortly after the
surrender of 1945, Hitler knew, from the "high point of the
start of 1942 on," that "victory was no longer attainable."[21]

Even now, however, Hitler held fast to the literal sense of the
alternative that had characterized his life's ambition in *Mein*
Kampf: "world power or decline." During the bloodiest winter
battles of the Eastern army, he told confidants on January 27,
1942: "Here too I am ice cold. If the German people are not prepared to stand up for their own preservation, fine. Then they
should perish."[22] Despite extreme, fanatical efforts in all spheres
of activity (political, military, economic, industrial, psychological) in Hitler's shrinking bastion from 1942 on, his aim of
German world power was beyond reach. And so his alternative
—the resolve not to capitulate but instead to bring about the deliberate destruction of Germany—led to that inferno of a war in
which not only the Reich's great power position was lost but, in
the end, German national unity itself was placed in dire peril.

In the same winter of 1941–1942 that witnessed the failure
of Hitler's war plans, Stalin decided that the moment had come
to reveal his own broad aims to the Anglo-Saxon powers. At the
time of the German attack on the Soviet Union, Great Britain
and the United States had, like Hitler, reckoned with a Soviet
collapse within a matter of weeks. They therefore did not commit themselves strongly to their new "partner" but concentrated
instead on adapting their global strategy against Germany and

Japan—conceived before the German attack on Russia—to the period after the expected Russian defeat. The world-shaking result of the summer and fall of 1941 was that Stalin withstood the crisis without having been forced into political dependency on Britain and America in order to gain effective Western assistance at a time when the Red Army repeatedly threatened to collapse. Stalin managed to defend the autonomous position of the Soviet Union—the prerequisite for the achievement of his own war aims and for the rise of the Soviet Union in power politics.

Thus, during his visit to Moscow on December 16–20, 1941, British Foreign Minister Eden found himself faced with the same ambitions—those of Stalin's long-term policy of security through strategic expansion—that Molotov had intimated to Hitler and Ribbentrop in November 1940 as the Soviet program for the final phase of the war. But now this policy was linked to the further goal of destroying the German Reich so that the situation of June 22, 1941, should never recur. At bottom, Stalin's aim represented but the obverse of Hitler's policy, which sought, by smashing the Soviet Union and erecting the four "Reich Commissariats," to guarantee that no strong power would ever again arise east of his continental empire bounded by the Urals.

After it became clear early on that England and America were not vitally concerned with Eastern Europe, the German Eastern army, like the peoples of Eastern Europe and later eastern Germany, found themselves caught in the inescapable, catastrophic bind between Hitler and Stalin. The unprecedented level of violence that this war of total destruction unleashed, first on the Soviet and then the German side, led to a bitter struggle of nearly four years in which millions perished. It ended only with Germany's unconditional surrender in 1945. As both sides, for different motives but with similar effect, struggled to annihilate the other, the Eastern war became, by a nearly inconceivable degree, the bloodiest in history. The nature of the struggle precluded an armistice of the kind that might end a "normal" European war. It ended instead with a German capitulation whose historical consequences extend far beyond the military event.

With the entry of the Red Army into the Eastern and Central European territory that Stalin had claimed as early as 1940–

1941 for a postwar bastion against the Western powers, there began the removal (vindicated in terms of both power politics and ideology) of the "class enemy." This term, adapted to the concept of the great "patriotic war," was directed against all "enemies of the Soviet Union" and led beyond the expulsion and deportation of whole peoples to the destruction of their very livelihood. All this served to establish the framework— geared to new alignments of power and the development of new military technology and strategy—for the long-term security of the Soviet Imperium.

From 1945 to the present, the essence of Soviet policy toward Germany and Europe has been the maintenance of the positions won in 1945. It has been determined by two closely entwined phenomena: the confrontation with the Anglo-Saxon powers in Central Europe, and the determination to hinder a repetition of the German attack. To the German mind, such a repetition seems unthinkable. But to the Soviets, traumatized by the experiences of June 22, 1941, it is the possible result of the unification of German potential in a single, great state, as between 1871 and 1945. Thus Hitlerian Germany's high share of responsibility for the Second World War and Imperial Germany's considerable, if somewhat more moderate, responsibility for the First World War together constitute a severe handicap for the political purpose of the present German Federal Republic, as published in the "Letter on German Unity" in conjunction with the German-Soviet treaty of August 12, 1970: "To work toward a condition of peace in Europe in which the German people, in free self-determination, may regain their unity."

NOTES

1. From Great Power Policy to World Policy

1. Max Weber, *Gesammelte politische Schriften*, ed. J. Winckelmann (Tübingen, 1958), p. 23. [All translations of quotations from German works are by William C. Kirby.] On Weber's political concerns see H. H. Gerth and C. Wright Mills, ed., *From Max Weber: Essays in Sociology* (New York: Oxford University Press, 1972), pp. 32–44.

2. Werner Frauendienst, *Das Deutsche Reich von 1890 bis 1914* (Constance, 1964), p. 99.

3. *Die grosse Politik der europäischen Kabinette, 1871–1914*, ed. Johannes Lepsius et al. (Berlin, 1922–), vol. II, no. 246, p. 64.

4. Frauendienst, *Das Deutsche Reich*, p. 125.

5. Fritz Dickmann, *Die Kriegsschuldfrage auf der Friedenskonferenz von Paris 1919*, Beiträge zur europäischen Geschichte, vol. 3 (Munich, 1964), p. 14.

2. The Return of the Great Powers to Europe

1. First published in Walther Hubatch, *Die Ära Tirpitz: Studien zur deutschen Marinepolitik, 1890–1918* (Göttingen, 1955), p. 92.

2. Wilhelm Widenmann, *Marine-Attaché an der Kaiserlich deutschen Botschaft in London, 1907–1912* (Göttingen, 1952), pp. 186–187.

3. Quoted in Oscar Freiherr von der Lanken-Wakewitz, *Meine dreissig Dienstjahre, 1888–1918* (Potsdam, Paris, and Brussels, 1931), pp. 56–57.

4. Wolfgang Foerster, review of Gerhard Ritter, *Der Schlieffen-Plan: Kritik eines Mythos* (Munich, 1956), in *Wehrwissenschaftliche Rundschau*, 7 (1957), 42–43.

5. Bernard Fürst von Bülow, *Denkwürdigkeiten* (Berlin, 1931), III, 241. Also available in English as *Memoirs of Prince von Bülow*, trans. Geoffrey Dunlop (Boston: Little, Brown, 1932), III, 269.

6. Alfred von Tirpitz, ed., *Politische Dokumente: Der Aufbau der deutschen Weltmacht* (Stuttgart and Berlin, 1924), p. 319.

7. *Die grosse Politik*, vol. IX, no. 2315, p. 353. Hatzfeld (London) to Holstein, June 18, 1895.

3. The German Leadership in the Crisis of July 1914

1. J. J. Ruedorffer (Kurt Riezler), *Grundzüge der Weltpolitik der Gegenwart* (Stuttgart and Berlin, 1914).

2. This and the following citations are from Ruedorffer, *Grundzüge*, pp. 214–232.

3. Egmont Zechlin, "Deutschland zwischen Kabinetts-krieg und Wirtschaftskrieg: Politik und Kriegführung in den ersten Monaten des Weltkrieges 1914," *Historische Zeitschrift*, 199 (1964), 400. Based on information from the Chancellor's son, Felix von Bethmann Hollweg.

4. Ruedorffer, *Grundzüge*, p. 226.

5. Karl Alexander von Müller, *Mars und Venus: Erinnerungen, 1914–1919* (Stuttgart, 1954), pp. 36–37.

6. Quoted in Gerhard Ritter, *Staatskunst und Kriegshandwerk: Das Problem des "Militarismus" in Deutschland* (Munich, 1960–), II, 269. Available in English as *The Sword and the Scepter: The Problem of Militarism in Germany*, trans. Heinz Norden (Coral Gables: University of Miami Press, 1970).

7. Ritter, *Staatskunst und Kriegshandwerk*, II, 270.

8. Walter Görlitz, ed., *Der Kaiser . . . Aufzeichnungen des Chefs des Marinekabinetts Admiral Georg Alexander von Müller über die Ära Wilhelms II* (Göttingen, 1965), p. 125.

9. Ibid.

10. Memorandum by Jagow, "Discussion with General von Moltke in the Spring of 1914" (May 20 or June 3, 1914), first published in Egmont Zechlin, "Motive und Taktik der Reichsleitung 1914," *Der Monat*, February 1966, p. 92.

11. Karl Dietrich Erdmann, "Zur Beurteilung Bethmann Hollwegs," *Geschichte in Wissenschaft und Unterricht*, 15 (1964), 536.

12. Tschirschky (Vienna) to Bethmann Hollweg, June 30, 1914

(with marginalia by William II), cited in Imanuel Geiss, ed., *Julikrise und Kriegsausbruch 1914* (Hanover, 1963), I, 59.

13. Erdmann, "Zur Beurteilung Bethmann Hollwegs," p. 536.

14. Theobald von Bethmann Hollweg, *Betrachtungen zum Weltkrieg* (Berlin, 1919), I, 133. Available in English as *Reflections on the World War*, trans. George Young (London, 1920).

15. Erdmann, "Zur Beurteilung Bethmann Hollwegs," p. 536.

16. Ruedorffer, *Grundzüge*, p. 222.

17. Erdmann, "Zur Beurteilung Bethmann Hollwegs," p. 536.

18. Ibid.

19. Ibid.

20. Ibid.

21. Bethmann Hollweg, *Betrachtungen*, II, 241ff.

22. Jagow to Lichnowsky, July 18, 1914, in Geiss, *Julikrise*, I, 208.

23. Jagow to Ballin, July 15, 1914, in Geiss, *Julikrise*, I, 176.

24. Zechlin, "Motive und Taktik der Reichsleitung," p. 92.

25. Ibid.

26. Ibid., p. 93.

27. Egmont Zechlin, "Bethmann Hollweg, Kriegsrisiko und SPD 1914," *Der Monat*, January 1966, p. 21.

28. Jagow to Lichnowsky, July 18, 1914, in Geiss, *Julikrise*, I, 208.

29. Ritter, *Staatskunst und Kriegshandwerk*, II, 113.

30. Telegram, Bethmann Hollweg to William II, July 26, 1914, first published in Zechlin, "Bethmann Hollweg, Kriegsrisiko und SPD 1914," p. 32.

31. Erdmann, "Zur Beurteilung Bethmann Hollwegs," p. 527.

32. William II to Jagow, July 28, 1914, in Geiss, *Julikrise*, II, 184–185.

33. Geiss, *Julikrise*, II, 373.

34. Erdmann, "Zur Beurteilung Bethmann Hollwegs," p. 536.

35. Zechlin, "Deutschland zwischen Kabinettskrieg und Wirtschaftskrieg," p. 403.

36. Quotation is from Max M. Warburg, *Aus meinen Aufzeichnungen* (1952) in Zechlin, "Bethmann Hollweg, Kriegsrisiko und SPD 1914," p. 20.

37. Bethmann Hollweg to Theodor Wolff, Feb. 5, 1915, cited in Karl-Heinz Janssen, *Der Kanzler und der General: Die Führungskrise um Bethmann Hollweg und Falkenhayn (1914–1916)* (Göttingen, 1967), p. 3.

38. Notes by Conrad Haussmann of his talk with Bethmann Hollweg of February 24, 1918, cited in Wolfgang Steglich, *Die Friedenspolitik der Mittelmächte, 1917–18* (Wiesbaden, 1964), p. 418.

4. New German Foreign Policy Objectives, 1914–1918

1. "Provisional Notes concerning the Direction of our Policy on the Conclusion of Peace" (Bethmann Hollweg's so-called September Program of September 9, 1914), with notes to Clemens von Delbrück and Arthur Zimmerman, published in Egmont Zechlin, "Friedensbestrebungen und Revolutionierungsversuche," in *Aus Politik und Zeitgeschichte*, supplement to *Das Parlament*, 20 (May 15, 1963), 41ff.

2. Bethmann Hollweg before the Prussian Staatsministerium, October 27, 1916, in Ritter, *Staatskunst und Kriegshandwerk*, III, 335.

3. Ludendorff at the German-Austro-Hungarian conference in Berlin, February 5, 1918, in Fritz Fischer, *Griff nach der Weltmacht: Die Kriegszielpolitik des kaiserlichen Deutschland, 1914–18*, 3rd. ed. (Düsseldorf, 1964), p. 659. Available in English as *Germany's Aims in the First World War* (New York: W. W. Norton, 1967).

4. Richard von Kühlmann, *Erinnerungen* (Heidelberg, 1948), p. 547.

5. Adolf Hitler, *Mein Kampf*, 12th ed. (Munich, 1943), pp. 741–742. Available in English under the same title, trans. Ralph Mannheim (Boston: Houghton Mifflin, 1943).

5. Hitler's Program

1. See Rudolph Binion, *Hitler among the Germans* (New York: Elsevier, 1976).

2. Gerhard L. Weinberg, ed., *Hitlers zweites Buch: Ein Dokument aus dem Jahr 1928*, Quellen und Darstellungen zur Zeitgeschichte, no. 7 (Stuttgart, 1961). Available in English as *Hitler's Secret Book*, trans. Salvator Attanasio, (New York: Grove Press, 1961).

3. *Hitlers zweites Buch*, p. 130.

4. Ibid., p. 128.

5. The derivation of this aspect of Hitler's program has now been precisely established by Binion, *Hitler among the Germans*, pp. 61–63, 78–82.

6. Hitler, *Mein Kampf*, p. 699.

7. Fritz Dickmann, "Machtwille und Ideologie in Hitlers Aussenpolitische Zielsetzung vor 1933," in *Spiegel der Geschichte: Festgabe für Max Braubach zum 10. 4. 1964* (Münster and Westfalen, 1964), pp. 920–921.

8. Jochen Thies, *Architekt der Weltherrschaft: Die "Endziele" Hitlers*, 2nd ed. (Düsseldorf, 1976), pp. 45–61.

6. Hitler's Foreign Policy and the Alignment of the Powers, 1933–1939

1. Goebbels' speech to invited members of the German press on April 5, 1940, excerpts in H. A. Jacobsen, *Der Zweite Weltkrieg: Grundzüge der Politik und Strategie in Dokumenten* (Frankfurt, 1965), pp. 180–181.

2. Notes by Lt. Gen. Liebmann on Hitler's speech to Reichswehr leaders on February 3, 1933, in *Vierteljahrshefte für Zeitgeschichte,* 1954, pp. 434–435.

3. Arnold J. Toynbee, *Acquaintances* (London, 1967), p. 282.

4. Bundesarchiv Koblenz, Sammlung Brammer, Goebbels' press instructions of March 16, 1939.

5. Bundesarchiv Koblenz, Akten des persönlichen Stabes Reichsführer SS, quoted in Hans Booms, "Der Ursprung des Zweiten Weltkrieges—Expansion oder Revision?" *Geschichte in Wissenschaft und Unterricht,* 1965, pp. 329ff.

6. Wilhelm Treue, "Hitlers Denkschrift zum Vierjahresplan 1936," *Vierteljahrshefte für Zeitgeschichte,* 1955, p. 210.

7. Rudolf Bogatsch, "Politische und militärische Probleme nach dem Frankreichfeldzug," in *Aus Politik und Zeitgeschichte,* supplement to *Das Parlament,* 1962, p. 176.

8. Goebbels to his closest colleagues at the end of the war on April 21, 1945, cited by Jürgen Thorwald, *Das Ende an der Elbe* (Stuttgart, 1950), p. 104.

9. Rolf Wagenführ, ed., *Die deutsche Industrie im Kriege* (Berlin, 1954), p. 24.

10. *Documents on German Foreign Policy, 1918–1945* (Washington, D.C.: U.S. Government Printing Office, 1960–), ser. D, vol. I, no. 423, pp. 655–656, Dieckhoff (Washington) to the German Foreign Ministry, December 7, 1937. This work will hereafter be cited as *DGFP.*

11. *DGFP,* ser. D, vol. I, no. 93, pp. 163–168, Ribbentrop, "Memorandum for the Führer," January 2, 1938.

7. Hitler, Stalin, and the British Government: August 1939

1. Carl J. Burckhardt, *Meine Danziger Mission, 1937–1939* (Munich, 1960), p. 348.

2. *DGFP,* ser. D, vol. VII, no. 265, pp. 280–281, unsigned memorandum, "Statement by the Führer to Henderson on August 25, 1939."

3. S. W. Roskill, *The War at Sea, 1939–1945* (London, 1954), I, 41.

4. R. J. M. Butler, *Grand Strategy* (London, 1957), II, 9–17.

5. *DGFP*, ser. D, vol. VII, no. 213, p. 227, unsigned record of the conversation on the night of August 23–24 between Ribbentrop, Stalin, and Molotov, Moscow, August 24, 1939.

6. J. W. Stalin, *Werke* (Berlin, 1952), VII, 11–12.

7. Hubertus Lupke, *Japans Russlandpolitik von 1939 bis 1941*, Schriften des Instituts für Asienkunde in Hamburg, vol. 10 (Frankfurt, 1962), p. 7. On the Nomonhan incident and Japan's attempt to come to terms with Russia, see pp. 7–24.

8. Elisabeth Wagner, ed., *Der Generalquartiermeister: Briefe und Tagebuchaufzeichnungen des Generalquartiermeisters des Heeres, General der Artillerie Eduard Wagner* (Munich and Vienna, 1963), p. 109.

9. Franz Halder, *Kriegstagebuch: Tägliche Aufzeichnungen des Chefs des Generalstabes des Heeres, 1939–1942*, ed. Hans-Adolf Jacobsen (Stuttgart, 1962), I, 42.

8. Hitler's Road to His War, 1940–1941

1. Halder, *Kriegstagebuch*, I, 375.

2. Ibid., p. 308.

3. Karl Klee, *Das Unternehmen "Seelöwe": Die geplante deutsche Landung in England 1940* (Göttingen, 1958), pp. 189–190.

4. Halder, *Kriegstagebuch*, II, 6.

5. Ibid.

6. Alfred Philippi, *Das Pripjetproblem: Eine Studie über die operative Bedeuting des Pripjets-Gebietes für den Feldzug des Jahres 1941* (Frankfurt, 1956), pp. 69ff. This was the first publication of large parts of the "Marcks Plan."

7. Halder, *Kriegstagebuch*, II, 210.

8. Communication from the former Chief of the Operations Department of the Army General Staff, Adolf Heusinger, to the Institut für Zeitgeschichte, Munich. See Andreas Hillgruber, *Hitlers Strategie: Politik und Kriegführung, 1940–1941* (Frankfurt, 1965), p. 273.

9. Halder, *Kriegstagebuch*, II. 203.

10. *DGFP*, ser. D, vol. XI, no. 438, p. 770, memorandum, "Conversation of the Führer with Bulgarian Minister Draganov," December 3, 1940.

11. Halder, *Kriegstagebuch*, II, 49.

12. *Akten zur deutschen auswärtigen Politik, 1918–1945* (Bonn,

1966–), ser. D, vol. XI, no. 329, p. 472, conversation between Ribbentrop and Molotov, November 13, 1940.

13. Butler, *Grand Strategy*, II, 543–544.

14. Halder, *Kriegstagebuch*, II, 335–338.

15. Hans-Adolf Jacobsen, "The *Kommissarbefehl* and Mass Executions of Soviet Russian Prisoners of War," in Hans Buchheim et al., *Anatomy of the SS State*, trans. R. Barry, M. Jackson, D. Long (New York: Walker and Company, 1968), p. 517.

16. Halder, *Kriegstagebuch*, II, 337.

17. Wagner, *Der Generalquartiermeister*, p. 202.

18. Politisches Archiv im Auswärtigen Amt, Bonn, filmed document no. 7/0119-0108, memorandum on conversation between Hitler and Kvaternik, July 21, 1941.

19. Nuremberg Document NO-2586, PS-710, photocopy at the Institut für Zeitgeschichte, Munich.

9. Hitler's World Policy from Triumph to Catastrophe

1. Halder, *Kriegstagebuch*, III, 38.

2. Walther Hubatsch, *Hitlers Weisungen für die Kriegsführung, 1939–1945: Dokumente des Oberkommandos der Wehrmacht* (Frankfurt, 1962), pp. 136ff.

3. *DGFP*, ser. D, vol. XIII, no. 89, pp. 112–113, Ribbentrop to Ott (Tokyo), July 10, 1941.

4. Andreas Hillgruber, ed., *Staatsmänner und Diplomaten bei Hitler: Vertrauliche Aufzeichnungen über Unterredungen mit Vertretern des Auslandes, 1939–1941* (Frankfurt, 1967), p. 606.

5. *Kriegstagebuch der Seekriegsleitung*, part C, book A (in Militärgeschichtliches Forschungsamt, Freiburg), memorandum of a discussion between Hitler and Raeder, July 25, 1941.

6. Hillgruber, *Staatsmänner und Diplomaten*, p. 608.

7. *Kriegstagebuch der Seekriegsleitung*, part C, book A, memorandum of a discussion between Hitler and Raeder, May 22, 1941.

8. Halder, *Kriegstagebuch*, III, 106–107.

9. *Kriegstagebuch des Oberkommandos der Wehrmacht (Wehrmachtführungsstab)*, gen. ed. Percy Ernst Schramm; vol. I (1940–1941), ed. Hans-Adolf Jacobsen (Frankfurt, 1965), p. 1021.

10. Halder, *Kriegstagebuch*, III, 53.

11. Alexander Dallin, *German Rule in Russia, 1941–1945: A Study of Occupation Policies* (New York: Macmillan, 1957), p. 59.

12. *DGFP*, ser. D, vol. XIII, no. 265, pp. 422–433, memorandum of the High Command of the Wehrmacht, "The Strategic Situation in

Late Summer 1941 as Basis for Further Political and Military Plans," August 27, 1941.

13. Henry Picker, *Hitlers Tischgespräche im Führerhauptquartier, 1941–42*, new ed. by Percy Ernst Schramm in collaboration with Andreas Hillgruber and Martin Vogt (Stuttgart, 1965), p. 145.

14. Hillgruber, *Staatsmänner und Diplomaten*, pp. 632–633.

15. Halder, *Kriegstagebuch*, III, 295.

16. Ibid., p. 306.

17. Egmont Zechlin, "Friedensbestrebungen und Revolutionierungsversuche," in *Aus Politik und Zeitgeschichte*, supplement to *Das Parlament*, 20 (1961), 275–276.

18. Halder, *Kriegstagebuch*, III, 333.

19. Hans-Adolf Jacobsen, *1939–1945: Der Zweite Weltkrieg in Chronik und Dokumenten* (Darmstadt, 1961), p. 290.

20. *Kriegstagebuch des Oberkommandos der Wehrmacht (Wehrmachtführungsstab)*, gen. ed. Percy Ernst Schramm; vol. II (1942), ed. Andreas Hillgruber (Frankfurt, 1963), pp. 1292ff.

21. Ibid., vol. IV (1944–1945), ed. Percy Ernst Schramm (Frankfurt, 1961), p. 1503.

22. Picker, *Hitlers Tischgespräche*, p. 171.

SELECTED BIBLIOGRAPHY

General Works

Bracher, Karl Dietrich. *Die Krise Europas, 1917–1975.* Vol. V, *Propyläen Geschichte Europas.* Berlin, 1976.
Calleo, David. *The German Problem Reconsidered: Germany and the World Order, 1870 to the Present.* New York, 1976.
Craig, Gordon A. *Germany, 1866–1945.* Oxford, 1978.
Dehio, Ludwig. *Germany and World Politics.* New York, 1959.
Fischer, Fritz. *Bündnis der Eliten: Zur Kontinuität der Machtstrukturen in Deutschland, 1871–1945.* Düsseldorf, 1979.
Hillgruber, Andreas. *Deutsche Grossmacht- und Weltpolitik im 19. und 20. Jahrhundert.* Düsseldorf, 1977.
———— *Grossmachtpolitik und Militarismus im 19. Jahrhundert: Drei Beiträge zum Kontinuitätsproblem.* Düsseldorf, 1979.
Ziebura, Gilbert, ed. *Grundfragen der deutschen Aussenpolitik seit 1871.* Wege zur Forschung, vol. 315. Darmstadt, 1975.

Works on German Policy before and during the First World War

Baumgart, Winfred. *Deutsche Ostpolitik 1918.* Munich, 1966.
———— *Deutschland im Zeitalter des Imperialismus.* Berlin, 1972.
Berghahn, Volker R. *Germany and the Approach of War in 1914.* London and New York, 1973.
———— *Rüstung und Machtpolitik: Zur Anatomie des "Kalten Krieges" vor 1914.* Düsseldorf, 1973.
———— *Der Tirpitz-Plan: Genesis und Verfall einer innenpolitischen Krisenstragetie unter Wilhelm II.* Düsseldorf, 1972.

Burchardt, Lothar. *Friedenswirtschaft und Kriegsvorsorge: Deutschlands wirtschaftliche Rüstungsbestrebungen vor 1914.* Boppard am Rhein, 1968.

Dickmann, Fritz. *Die Kriegsschuldfrage auf der Friedenskonferenz von Paris 1919.* Munich, 1964.

Erdmann, Karl Dietrich. *Die Zeit der Weltkriege.* Vol. IV, part 1, *Gebhardt Handbuch der deutschen Geschichte,* 9th ed. Stuttgart, 1973.

—— "Zur Beurteilung Bethmann Hollwegs." *Geschichte in Wissenschaft und Unterricht,* 16 (1974), 525ff.

Erdmann, Karl Dietrich, ed. *Kurt Riezler: Tagebücher, Aufsätze, Dokumente.* Göttingen, 1972.

Fischer, Fritz. *Der Erste Weltkrieg und das deutsche Geschichtsbild: Beiträge zur Bewältigung eines historischen Tabus.* Düsseldorf, 1977.

—— *Germany's Aims in the First World War.* New York, 1967.

—— *War of Illusions: German Policies from 1911 to 1914.* New York, 1975.

Frauendienst, Werner, and Wolfgang J. Mommsen. *Das Deutsche Reich von 1890 bis 1914.* Vol. IV, *Handbuch der deutschen Geschichte,* ed. Otto Brandt, A. O. Meyer, and Leo Just. Constance and Frankfurt, 1963–1973.

Geiss, Imanuel. *Das Deutsche Reich und der Erste Weltkrieg.* Munich, 1978.

—— *Das Deutsche Reich und die Vorgeschichte des Ersten Weltkrieges.* Munich, 1978.

—— *German Foreign Policy, 1871–1914.* London, 1976.

Haupts, Leo. *Deutsche Friedenspolitik, 1918–19: Eine Alternative zur Machtpolitik des Ersten Weltkrieges.* Düsseldorf, 1976.

Herzfeld, Hans. *Der Erste Weltkrieg.* 3rd. ed. Munich, 1974.

Hildebrand, Klaus. *Bethmann Hollweg, Der Kanzler ohne Eigenschaften: Eine kritische Bibliographie.* Düsseldorf, 1971.

—— "Imperialismus, Wettrüsten und Kriegsausbruch 1914." *Neue Politische Literatur,* 20 (1975), 160–194, 339–364.

Hölzle, Erwin. *Die Selbstentmachung Europas.* 2 vols. Göttingen, Frankfurt, and Zürich, 1978.

Janssen, Karl-Heinz. *Der Kanzler und der General: Die Führungskrise um Bethmann Hollweg und Falkenhayn (1914–1916).* Göttingen, Frankfurt, and Zürich, 1967.

Jarausch, Konrad H. *The Enigmatic Chancellor: Bethmann Hollweg and the Hubris of Imperial Germany.* New Haven, 1973.

Kielmannsegg, Peter, Graf von. *Deutschland und der Erste Weltkrieg.* Frankfurt, 1968.

Laqueur, Walter and George Mosse, eds. *1914: The coming of the First World War.* New York, 1966.

Mommsen, Wolfgang J. "Europäischer Finanzimperialismus vor 1914: Ein Beitrag zu einer pluralistischen Theorie des Imperialismus." *Historische Zeitschrift,* 224 (1977), 17–81.

——— *Das Zeitalter des Imperialismus.* Frankfurt, 1969.

Moses, John A. *The Politics of Illusion: The Fischer Controversy in German Historiography.* London, 1975.

Raulff, Heiner. *Zwischen Machtpolitik und Imperialismus: Die deutsche Frankreichpolitik, 1904–1906.* Düsseldorf, 1976.

Ritter, Gerhard. *The Sword and the Scepter: The Problem of Militarism in Germany.* Trans. Heinz Norden. Coral Gables, Fla., 1969–1973.

Röhl, John C. G. "Die Generalprobe: Zur Geschichte und Bedeutung des 'Kriegsrates' vom. 8. Dezember 1912." In *Industrielle Gesellschaft und politisches System,* ed. D. Stegmann et al. (Bonn, 1978), pp. 357ff.

Schieder, Theodor. *Europa im Zeitalter der Nationalstaaten und Europäische Weltpolitik bis zum Ersten Weltkrieg.* Vol. VI, *Handbuch der europäischen Geschichte,* ed. Theodor Schieder. Stuttgart, 1968.

——— *Staatensystem als Vormacht der Welt, 1848–1918.* Vol. V, *Propyläen Geschichte Europas.* Berlin, 1977.

Schieder, Wolfgang, ed. *Erster Weltkrieg: Ursachen, Entstehung und Kriegsziele.* Cologne, 1969.

Schwabe, Klaus. *Deutsche Revolution und Wilson-Frieden: Die amerikanische und deutsche Friedensstrategie zwischen Ideologie und Machtpolitik, 1918–19.* Düsseldorf, 1971.

Steinberg, Jonathan. *Yesterday's Deterrent: Tirpitz and the Birth of the German Battle Fleet.* New York, 1965.

Stürmer, Michael, ed. *Das Kaiserliche Deutschland: Politik und Gesellschaft, 1870–1918.* Düsseldorf, 1970.

Vogel, Barbara. *Deutsche Russlandpolitik: Das Scheitern der deutschen Weltpolitik unter Bülow, 1900–1906.* Düsseldorf, 1973.

Wehler, Hans-Ulrich. *Das Deutsche Kaiserreich, 1871–1918.* Göttingen, 1977.

Weitowitz, R. *Deutsche Politik und Handelspolitik unter Reichskanzler Leo von Caprivi, 1890–1894.* Düsseldorf, 1978.

Wintzen, Peter. *Bülows Weltmachtkonzept: Untersuchungen zur*

Frühphase seiner Aussenpolitik, 1897–1901. Boppard am Rhein, 1977.

———. "Die Englandpolitik Friedrich von Holsteins, 1895 bis 1901." Diss., University of Cologne, 1975.

Zechlin, Egmont. *Die deutsche Politik und die Juden im Ersten Weltkrieg.* Göttingen, 1969.

——— *Krieg und Kriegsrisiko: Zur deutschen Politik im Ersten Weltkrieg.* Düsseldorf, 1979.

Works on Hitler, National Socialism, and German Foreign Policy, 1919–1941.

Bracher, Karl Dietrich. *The German Dictatorship: The Origins, Structure, and Effects of National Socialism.* Trans. Jean Steinberg. New York, 1970.

Bariety, Jacques. *Les relations franco-allemandes après la première guerre mondiale.* Paris, 1977.

Bezymenskii, Lev. *Sonderakte "Barbarossa": Dokumente, Darstellung, Deutung.* Stuttgart, 1978.

Binion, Rudolph. *Hitler among the Germans.* New York, 1976.

Broszat, Martin. *Nationalsozialistische Polenpolitik, 1939–1945.* Stuttgart, 1961.

Buchheim, Hans, et al. *Anatomy of the SS State.* Trans. Richard Barry et al. New York, 1968.

Bullock, Alan. *Hitler: A Study in Tyranny.* 2nd ed. New York, 1962.

Carr, William. *Arms, Autarky, and Aggression: A Study in German Foreign Policy, 1933–1939.* London, 1972.

——— *Hitler: A Study in Personality and Politics.* London, 1978.

Conze, Werner. "Deutschlands weltpolitische Sonderstellung in den zwanziger Jahren." *Vierteljahrshefte für Zeitgeschichte,* 9 (1961), 166–177.

Conze, Werner, and H. Raupach, eds. *Die Staats- und Wirtschaftskrise des Deutschen Reiches, 1929–33.* Stuttgart, 1967.

Dallin, Alexander. *German Rule in Russia, 1941–1945: A Study of Occupation Policies.* New York, 1957.

Dülffer, Jost. *Weimar, Hitler und die Marine: Reichspolitik und Flottenbau, 1920–1939.* Düsseldorf, 1973.

Erdmann, Karl Dietrich. *Die Zeit der Weltkriege.* Vol. IV, part 2, *Gebhardt Handbuch der deutschen Geschichte,* 9th ed. Stuttgart, 1976.

Fabry, Phillip W. *Der Hitler-Stalin-Pakt, 1939–1941.* Darmstadt, 1962.

—— *Die Sowjetunion und das Dritte Reich: Eine Dokumentierte Geschichte der deutsch-sowjetischen Beziehungen von 1933 bis 1941.* Stuttgart, 1971.

Fest, Joachim C. *Hitler.* Trans. Richard and Clara Winston. New York, 1974.

Forndran, Erhard et al. *Innen- und Aussenpolitik unter nationalsozialistischer Bedrohung.* Opladen, 1977.

Funke, Manfred, ed. *Hitler, Deutschland und die Mächte: Materialien zur Aussenpolitik des Dritten Reiches.* Düsseldorf, 1976.

Henke, Josef. *England in Hitlers politischem Kalkül, 1935–1939.* Boppard am Rhein, 1973.

Hildebrand, Klaus. *The Foreign Policy of the Third Reich.* Trans. Anthony Fothergill. Berkeley, 1973.

—— "Hitlers Ort in der Geschichte des preussisch-deutschen Nationalstaates." *Historische Zeitschrift,* 217 (1973), 584–632.

—— *Vom Reich zum Weltreich: Hitler, NSDAP und koloniale Frage, 1919–1945.* Munich, 1969.

Hillgruber, Andreas. *Hitlers Strategie: Politik und Kriegführung 1940 bis 1941.* Frankfurt, 1965.

—— *Der Zenit des Zweiten Weltkrieges: Juli 1941.* Wiesbaden, 1977.

Hofer, Walther. *Die Diktatur Hitlers bis zum Beginn des Zweiten Weltkrieges, 1933–1939.* Vol. IV, *Handbuch der deutschen Geschichte,* ed. Otto Brandt, A. O. Meyer, and Leo Just. Constance, 1971.

—— *Die Entfesselung des Zweiten Weltkrieges.* 3rd ed. Frankfurt, 1964.

Hoggan, David L. *Der erzwungene Krieg.* Tübingen, 1961, 1974.

Jäckel, Eberhard. *Frankreich in Hitlers Europa.* Stuttgart, 1966.

—— *Hitler's Weltanschauung: A Blueprint For Power.* Trans. Herbert Arnold. Middletown, Conn., 1972.

Jacobsen, Hans-Adolf. *Nationalsozialistische Aussenpolitik, 1933–38.* Frankfurt, 1968.

—— *Von der Strategie der Gewalt zur Politik der Friedenssicherung: Beiträge zur deutschen Geschichte im 20. Jahrhundert.* Düsseldorf, 1977.

—— *Der Weg zur Teilung der Welt: Politik und Strategie 1939 bis 1945.* Coblenz and Bonn, 1977.

Kuhn, Axel. *Hitlers aussenpolitisches Programm: Entstehung und Entwicklung, 1919–1939.* Stuttgart, 1970.

Lukacs, John A. *The Last European War: September 1939–December 1941.* London, 1976.

112 Selected Bibliography

Martin, Bernd. *Deutschland und Japan im Zweiten Weltkrieg*. Göttingen, Zürich, and Frankfurt, 1969.
——— *Friedensinitiativen und Machtpolitik im Zweiten Weltkrieg, 1939–1942*. Düsseldorf, 1976.
Maxelon, Michael-Olaf. *Stresemann und Frankreich: Deutsche Politik der Ost-West-Balance*. Düsseldorf, 1972.
Metzmacher, Helmuth. "Deutsch-englische Ausgleichsbemühungen im Sommer 1939." *Vierteljahrshefte für Zeitgeschichte*, 14 (1966), 369–412.
Michalka, Wolfgang, ed. *Nationalsozialistische Aussenpolitik*. Wege der Forschung, vol. 297. Darmstadt, 1978.
Moltmann, Günter. "Deutschland und die Welt im Jahre 1939." In *Schicksalsjahre deutscher Geschichte, 1914–1939–1944*, ed. K.-J. Müller (Boppard am Rhein, 1964).
——— "Weltherrschaftsideen Hitlers." In *Europa und Übersee: Festschrift für E. Zechlin* (Hamburg, 1961), pp. 197ff.
Niedhart, Gottfried, ed. *Kriegsbeginn 1939: Entfesselung oder Ausbruch des Zweiten Weltkrieges?* Wege der Forschung, vol. 374. Darmstadt, 1976.
Petersen, Jens. *Hitler-Mussolini: Die Entstehung der Achse Berlin-Rom, 1933–1936*. Tübingen, 1973.
Rich, Norman. *Hitler's War Aims*. 2 vols. New York, 1973–1974.
Salewski, Michael. *Die deutsche Seekriegsleitung, 1935–1945*. 3 vols. Frankfurt and Munich, 1970–1975.
Schubert, Gunther. *Anfänge nationalsozialistischer Aussenpolitik*. Cologne, 1962.
Siebert, Ferdinand. *Italiens Weg in den Zweiten Weltkrieg*. Frankfurt, 1962.
Streit, Christian. *Keine Kameraden: Die Wehrmacht und die sowjetischen Kriegsgefangenen, 1941–1945*. Stuttgart, 1978.
Sommer, Theo. *Deutschland und Japan zwischen den Mächten 1935 bis 1940*. Tübingen, 1962.
Speer, Albert. *Inside the Third Reich*. Trans. Richard and Clara Winston. New York, 1970.
——— *Spandau: The Secret Diaries*. Trans. Richard and Clara Winston. New York, 1976.
Taylor, A. J. P. *The Origins of the Second World War*. London, 1961.
Thies, Jochen. *Architekt der Weltherrschaft: Die "Endziele" Hitlers*. Düsseldorf, 1976.
Trevor-Roper, H. R. "Hitlers Kriegziele." In *Stationen der deutschen Geschichte, 1919–1945*, ed. B. Freudenfeld (Stuttgart, 1962), pp. 9ff.

Weinberg, Gerhard L. *The Foreign Policy of Hitler's Germany: Diplomatic Revolution in Europe, 1933–36.* Chicago, 1970.

Weizsäcker, Ernst von. *Die Weizsäcker-Papiere, 1933–1950.* Ed. L. E. Hill. Frankfurt, 1974.

Wollstein, Günter. *Vom Weimarer Revisionismus zu Hitler: Das Deutsche Reich und die Grossmächte in der Anfangsphase der nationalsozialistischen Herrschaft in Deutschland.* Bonn-Bad Godesberg, 1973.

INDEX

Abyssinia, Italy's war in, 59
Afghanistan, 89, 94
Africa: Anglo-German rivalry in, 8–9, 21: Hitler's aims in, 50, 53, 89, 90; demand for return of German colonies in, 61
Air force, Hitler's plans for, 90
Algeciras Conference, 17
Alsace-Loraine, 3–4
Anglo-French agreement (1939), 71; discussions on possible strategy under, 71–72
Anglo-German alliance negotiations (1898–1901), 11
Anglo-German Naval Agreement (1935), 59; Hitler's abrogation of, 61–62
Anglo-Russian settlement (1907), 19
Anti-Comintern Pact (1936), 67
Anti-Semitism: of Hitler, 49; related to foreign policy, 49–51
Appeasement, foreign policy based on, 60
Archangel, 89
Arms race, Anglo-German (1908–1911), 15, 17
Aryans, Hitler on, 51
Astrakhan, 89
Atlantic Ocean, sea lanes crucial to Britain, 70–71
Austria: pan-German agitation in, 53; withdrawal from League, 59; incorporation of, 63

Austria-Hungary: German alliance with, 3, 4, 19; and the Balkans, 20, 25–26; as "stagnating power," 24–26; and attack on Serbia, 31–33, 36–37, 39
Axis Powers, 65; in Spain, 59
Azores, 92

Baghdad, railway from Berlin to, 10, 21
Baku oil region, 84
Balkan War (1913–1914), 25
Balkans, 19, 20–21; Riezler on diplomacy toward, 24; Austria's stake in, 25–26; Moltke's strategy toward, 28–29; and start of World War I, 39–40
Ballin, Albert, 33
Baltic Sea, 83, 84
Baltic states, 86
"Basic Characteristics of Present Day World Politics" (Riezler), 22–23
Belgian Congo, 21
Belgium, 8, 17, 27–28
Belgrade, 35, 36
Berlin-Rome-Tokyo triangle, Ribbentrop on, 65, 67
Bernhardi, Friedrich von, 48
Bethmann Hollweg, Theobald von, 5, 14, 18, 19, 25, 94; 1912 statement by, 19–20; strategy toward England and Russia, 20–21, 26–27, 29–30; on Serbia, 30, 31–32, 34–36; loss of control of crisis by, 36–37, 39; fall